MznLnx

Missing Links Exam Preps

Exam Prep for

Finite Mathematics

Waner, Costenoble, 3rd Edition

The MznLnx Exam Prep is your link from the textbook and lecture to your exams.
The MznLnx Exam Preps are unauthorized and comprehensive reviews of your textbooks.

All material provided by MznLnx and Rico Publications (c) 2010
Textbook publishers and textbook authors do not particpate in or contribute to these reviews.

MznLnx

Rico
Publications

Exam Prep for Finite Mathematics
3rd Edition
Waner, Costenoble

Publisher: Raymond Houge	*Product Manager:* Dave Mason
Assistant Editor: Michael Rouger	*Editorial Assitant:* Rachel Guzmanji
Text and Cover Designer: Lisa Buckner	*Pedagogy:* Debra Long
Marketing Manager: Sara Swagger	*Cover Image:* Jim Reed/Getty Images
Project Manager, Editorial Production: Jerry Emerson	*Text and Cover Printer:* City Printing, Inc.
Art Director: Vernon Lowerui	*Compositor:* Media Mix, Inc.

(c) 2010 Rico Publications

ALL RIGHTS RESERVED. No part of this work covered by the copyright may be reproduced or used in any form or by an means--graphic, electronic, or mechanical, including photocopying, recording, taping, Web distribution, information storage, and retrieval systems, or in any other manner--without the written permission of the publisher.

Printed in the United States
ISBN:

For more information about our products, contact us at:

Dave.Mason@RicoPublications.com

For permission to use material from this text or product, submit a request online to:

Dave.Mason@RicoPublications.com

Contents

CHAPTER 1
FUNCTIONS AND LINEAR MODELS — 1

CHAPTER 2
SYSTEMS OF LINEAR EQUATIONS AND MATRICES — 19

CHAPTER 3
MATRIX ALGEBRA AND APPLICATIONS — 35

CHAPTER 4
LINEAR PROGRAMMING — 51

CHAPTER 5
THE MATHEMATICS OF FINANCE — 67

CHAPTER 6
SETS AND COUNTING — 76

CHAPTER 7
PROBABILITY — 89

CHAPTER 8
RANDOM VARIABLES AND STATISTICS — 104

CHAPTER 9
MARKOV SYSTEMS — 124

ANSWER KEY — 131

TO THE STUDENT

COMPREHENSIVE

The *MznLnx* Exam Prep series is designed to help you pass your exams. Editors at MznLnx review your textbooks and then prepare these practice exams to help you master the textbook material. Unlike study guides, workbooks, and practice tests provided by the texbook publisher and textbook authors, *MznLnx* gives you **all** of the material in each chapter in exam form, not just samples, so you can be sure to nail your exam.

MECHANICAL

The MznLnx Exam Prep series creates exams that will help you learn the subject matter as well as test you on your understanding. Each question is designed to help you master the concept. Just working through the exams, you gain an understanding of the subject--its a simple mechanical process that produces success.

INTEGRATED STUDY GUIDE AND REVIEW

MznLnx is not just a set of exams designed to test you, its also a comprehensive review of the subject content. Each exam question is also a review of the concept, making sure that you will get the answer correct without having to go to other sources of material. You learn as you go! Its the easiest way to pass an exam.

HUMOR

Studying can be tedious and dry. MznLnx's instructional design includes moderate humor within the exam questions on occassion, to break the tedium and revitalize the brain

Chapter 1. FUNCTIONS AND LINEAR MODELS

1. In statistics, _____ is a form of regression analysis in which the relationship between one or more independent variables and another variable, called dependent variable, is modeled by a least squares function, called _____ equation. This function is a linear combination of one or more model parameters, called regression coefficients. A _____ equation with one independent variable represents a straight line.
    a. Random variables
    b. Kurtosis
    c. Percentile rank
    d. Linear regression

2. The _____ fallacy is an informal fallacy. It ascribes cause where none exists. The flaw is failing to account for natural fluctuations.
    a. Degrees of freedom
    b. Regression
    c. Differential
    d. Depth

3. The mathematical concept of a _____ expresses the intuitive idea of deterministic dependence between two quantities, one of which is viewed as primary and the other as secondary. A _____ then is a way to associate a unique output for each input of a specified type, for example, a real number or an element of a given set.
    a. Coherent
    b. Going up
    c. Grill
    d. Function

4. _____ and independent variables refer to values that change in relationship to each other. The _____ are those that are observed to change in response to the independent variables. The independent variables are those that are deliberately manipulated to invoke a change in the _____.
    a. Round robin test
    b. Dependent variables
    c. Steiner system
    d. Yates analysis

5. In mathematics, especially in the area of abstract algebra known as ring theory, a _____ is a ring with $0 \neq 1$ such that $ab = 0$ implies that either $a = 0$ or $b = 0$. That is, it is a nontrivial ring without left or right zero divisors. A commutative _____ is called an integral _____.

Chapter 1. FUNCTIONS AND LINEAR MODELS

a. Left primitive ring
b. Modular representation theory
c. Simple ring
d. Domain

6. Dependent variables and _____ refer to values that change in relationship to each other. The dependent variables are those that are observed to change in response to the _____. The _____ are those that are deliberately manipulated to invoke a change in the dependent variables.

a. Operational confound
b. One-factor-at-a-time method
c. Experimental design diagram
d. Independent variables

7. _____ is a method of constructing new data points from a discrete set of known data points.

a. Archimedes' use of infinitesimals
b. Integration by substitution
c. Uniform convergence
d. Interpolation

8. In abstract algebra, a field extension L /K is called _____ if every element of L is _____ over K. Field extensions which are not _____.

For example, the field extension R/Q, that is the field of real numbers as an extension of the field of rational numbers, is transcendental, while the field extensions C/R and Q

a. Identity
b. Algebraic
c. Echo
d. Ideal

9. In statistics, given a sample $(Y_i, X_{i1}, \ldots, X_{ip})$, $i = 1, \ldots, n$ the most general form of _____ is formulated as

$$Y_i = \beta_0 + \beta_1 \phi_1(X_{i1}) + \ldots + \beta_p \phi_p(X_{ip}) + \varepsilon_i \qquad i = 1, \ldots, n$$

where $\phi_1, \ldots, \phi_p$ may be nonlinear functions.

In matrix notation this model can be written as

$$Y = X\beta + \varepsilon$$

where Y is an n × 1 column vector, X is an n × matrix, β is a × 1 vector of parameters, and ε is an n × 1 vector of errors, which are uncorrelated random variables each with expected value 0 and variance σ². Note that depending on the context the sample can be seen as fixed, or random.

a. Linear model
b. Risk measure
c. Life table
d. Risk aversion

10. In ecology, predation describes a biological interaction where a _____ (an organism that is hunting) feeds on its prey, the organism that is attacked. _____s may or may not kill their prey prior to feeding on them, but the act of predation always results in the death of the prey. The other main category of consumption is detritivory, the consumption of dead organic material (detritus.)

a. Prey
b. 1-center problem
c. 120-cell
d. Predator

11. In mathematics, the _____ is a direct product of sets. The _____ is named after René Descartes, whose formulation of analytic geometry gave rise to this concept.

Specifically, the _____ of two sets X and Y, denoted X × Y, is the set of all possible ordered pairs whose first component is a member of X and whose second component is a member of Y:

$$X \times Y = \{(x, y) | x \in X \text{ and } y \in Y\}.$$

For example, the _____ of the 13-element set of standard playing card ranks {Ace, King, Queen, Jack, 10, 9, 8, 7, 6, 5, 4, 3, 2} and the four-element set of card suits {♠, ♥, ♦, ♣} is the 52-element set of all possible playing cards ,, ...,, ...,}.

a. Disjoint sets
b. Set of all sets
c. Choice function
d. Cartesian product

12. A _____ typically refers to a class of handheld calculators that are capable of plotting graphs, solving simultaneous equations, and performing numerous other tasks with variables. Most popular _____s are also programmable, allowing the user to create customized programs, typically for scientific/engineering and education applications. Due to their large displays intended for graphing, they can also accommodate several lines of text and calculations at a time.

a. Genus
b. Support vector machines
c. Bump mapping
d. Graphing calculator

13. _____ or amortisation is the process of decreasing an amount over a period of time. The word comes from Middle English amortisen to kill, alienate in mortmain, from Anglo-French amorteser, alteration of amortir, from Vulgar Latin admortire to kill, from Latin ad- + mort-, mors death. Particular instances of the term include:

- _____, the allocation of a lump sum amount to different time periods, particularly for loans and other forms of finance, including related interest or other finance charges.
    - _____ schedule, a table detailing each periodic payment on a loan, as generated by an _____ calculator.
    - Negative _____, an _____ schedule where the loan amount actually increases through not paying the full interest
- Amortized analysis, analyzing the execution cost of algorithms over a sequence of operations.
- _____ of capital expenditures of certain assets under accounting rules, particularly intangible assets, in a manner analogous to depreciation.
- _____

_____ is also used in the context of zoning regulations and describes the time in which a property owner has to relocate when the property's use constitutes a preexisting nonconforming use under zoning regulations.

- Depreciation

a. Origin
b. Identity
c. ISAAC
d. Amortization

14. An _____ is a table detailing each periodic payment on a amortizing loan, as generated by an amortization calculator.

While a portion of every payment is applied towards both the interest and the principal balance of the loan, the exact amount applied to principal each time varies. An _____ reveals the specific monetary amount put towards interest, as well as the specific put towards the Principal balance, with each payment.

Chapter 1. FUNCTIONS AND LINEAR MODELS 5

a. A Mathematical Theory of Communication
b. A chemical equation
c. Amortization schedule
d. Accounts receivable

15. A _____ is a device for performing mathematical calculations, distinguished from a computer by having a limited problem solving ability and an interface optimized for interactive calculation rather than programming. _____s can be hardware or software, and mechanical or electronic, and are often built into devices such as PDAs or mobile phones.

Modern electronic _____s are generally small, digital, and usually inexpensive.

a. 2-3 heap
b. 1-center problem
c. 120-cell
d. Calculator

16. In mathematics, a _____ is a function whose definition is dependent on the value of the independent variable. Mathematically, a real-valued function f of a real variable x is a relationship whose definition is given differently on disjoint subsets of its domain

The word piecewise is also used to describe any property of a _____ that holds for each piece but may not hold for the whole domain of the function.

a. High-dimensional model representation
b. Surjective
c. Glide reflection
d. Piecewise-defined function

17. In mathematics, an _____ is informally a function which satisfies a polynomial equation whose coefficients are themselves polynomials. For example, an _____ in one variable x is a solution y for an equation

$$a_n(x)y^n + a_{n-1}(x)y^{n-1} + \cdots + a_0(x) = 0$$

where the coefficients a_i

Chapter 1. FUNCTIONS AND LINEAR MODELS

a. Algebraic signal processing
b. Algebraic solution
c. Alternatization
d. Algebraic function

18. In mathematics, a _____ is a function of the form

$$f3 + bx^2 + cx + d,$$

where a is nonzero; or in other words, a polynomial of degree three. The derivative of a _____ is a quadratic function. The integral of a _____ is a quartic function.

a. Quadratic equation
b. Linear equation
c. Quartic equation
d. Cubic function

19. The _____ is a function in mathematics. The application of this function to a value x is written as ex. Equivalently, this can be written in the form e^x, where e is a mathematical constant, the base of the natural logarithm, which equals approximately 2.718281828, and is also known as Euler's number.

a. A chemical equation
b. Area hyperbolic functions
c. A Mathematical Theory of Communication
d. Exponential function

20. In mathematics, a _____ is a system which is not linear. Less technically, a _____ is any problem where the variabl to be solved for cannot be written as a linear sum of independent components. A nonhomogenous system, which is linear apart from the presence of a function of the independent variables, is nonlinear according to a strict definition, but such systems are usually studied alongside linear systems, because they can be transformed to a linear system as long as a particular solution is known.

a. 1-center problem
b. Metric system
c. George Dantzig
d. Nonlinear system

Chapter 1. FUNCTIONS AND LINEAR MODELS

21. In mathematics, a _____ is an expression constructed from variables and constants, using the operations of addition, subtraction, multiplication, and constant non-negative whole number exponents. For example, $x^2 - 4x + 7$ is a _____, but $x^2 - 4/x + 7x^{3/2}$ is not, because its second term involves division by the variable x and also because its third term contains an exponent that is not a whole number.

_____s are one of the most important concepts in algebra and throughout mathematics and science.

a. Semifield
b. Coimage
c. Polynomial
d. Group extension

22. A _____, in mathematics, is a polynomial function of the form $f(x) = ax^2 + bx + c$, where $a \neq 0$. The graph of a _____ is a parabola whose major axis is parallel to the y-axis.

The expression $ax^2 + bx + c$ in the definition of a _____ is a polynomial of degree 2 or a 2nd degree polynomial, because the highest exponent of x is 2.

a. Laguerre polynomials
b. Multivariate division algorithm
c. Discriminant
d. Quadratic function

23. In mathematics, a _____ is any function which can be written as the ratio of two polynomial functions. _____ of degree 2 :

$$y = \frac{x^2 - 3x - 2}{x^2 - 4}$$

In the case of one variable, x, a _____ is a function of the form

$$f(x) = \frac{P(x)}{Q(x)}$$

where P and Q are polynomial function in x and Q is not the zero polynomial. The domain of f is the set of all points x for which the denominator Q

a. 120-cell
b. Rational function
c. 1-center problem
d. Legendre rational functions

24. _____ involves reducing the number of significant digits in a number. The result of _____ is a 'shorter' number having fewer non-zero digits yet similar in magnitude. The result is less precise but easier to use.
   a. Sudan function
   b. Hyper operator
   c. Rounding
   d. Shabakh

25. In mathematics, _____ and undefined are used to explain whether or not expressions have meaningful, sensible, and unambiguous values. Not all branches of mathematics come to the same conclusion.

The following expressions are undefined in all contexts, but remarks in the analysis section may apply.

   a. LHS
   b. Toy model
   c. Plugging in
   d. Defined

26. In mathematics, the _____ is a conic section, the intersection of a right circular conical surface and a plane parallel to a generating straight line of that surface. Given a point and a line that lie in a plane, the locus of points in that plane that are equidistant to them is a _____.

A particular case arises when the plane is tangent to the conical surface of a circle.

   a. Dandelin sphere
   b. Directrix
   c. Matrix representation of conic sections
   d. Parabola

27. In geometry, a _____ is a special kind of point, usually a corner of a polygon, polyhedron, or higher dimensional polytope. In the geometry of curves a _____ is a point of where the first derivative of curvature is zero. In graph theory, a _____ is the fundamental unit out of which graphs are formed

Chapter 1. FUNCTIONS AND LINEAR MODELS

a. Crib
b. Dini
c. Duality
d. Vertex

28. In mathematics, a _____ of a number x is a number r such that r^2 = x, or, in other words, a number r whose square is x. Every non-negative real number x has a unique non-negative _____, called the principal _____, which is denoted with a radical symbol as $\sqrt{x}$, or, using exponent notation, as $x^{1/2}$. For example, the principal _____ of 9 is 3, denoted $\sqrt{9}$ = 3, because 3^2 = 3 × 3 = 9.
   a. Square root
   b. Hyperbolic functions
   c. Double exponential
   d. Multiplicative inverse

29. In vascular plants, the _____ is the organ of a plant body that typically lies below the surface of the soil. This is not always the case, however, since a _____ can also be aerial (that is, growing above the ground) or aerating (that is, growing up above the ground or especially above water.) Furthermore, a stem normally occurring below ground is not exceptional either
   a. 2-3 heap
   b. 1-center problem
   c. 120-cell
   d. Root

30. In mathematics, an average, or _____ of a data set refers to a measure of the 'middle' or 'expected' value of the data set. There are many different descriptive statistics that can be chosen as a measurement of the _____ of the data items.

An average is a single value that is meant to typify a list of values.

   a. Mean reciprocal rank
   b. Quartile
   c. Central tendency
   d. Trimean

31. _____ is used to describe the steepness, incline, gradient, or grade of a straight line. A higher _____ value indicates a steeper incline. The _____ is defined as the ratio of the 'rise' divided by the 'run' between two points on a line, or in other words, the ratio of the altitude change to the horizontal distance between any two points on the line.

a. Number line
b. Point plotting
c. Cognitively Guided Instruction
d. Slope

32. A _____ is an algebraic equation in which each term is either a constant or the product of a constant and a single variable. _____s can have one, two, three or more variables.

_____s occur with great regularity in applied mathematics.

a. Difference of two squares
b. Quartic equation
c. Linear equation
d. Quadratic equation

33. In mathematics and in the sciences, a _____ (plural: _____e, formulæ or _____s) is a concise way of expressing information symbolically (as in a mathematical or chemical _____), or a general relationship between quantities. One of many famous _____e is Albert Einstein's $E = mc^2$ (see special relativity

In mathematics, a _____ is a key to solve an equation with variables. For example, the problem of determining the volume of a sphere is one that requires a significant amount of integral calculus to solve.

a. 1-center problem
b. 2-3 heap
c. 120-cell
d. Formula

34. In mathematics, a _____ is a rectangular table of elements, which may be numbers or, more generally, any abstract quantities that can be added and multiplied. Matrices are used to describe linear equations, keep track of the coefficients of linear transformations and to record data that depend on multiple parameters. Matrices are described by the field of _____ theory.
a. Compression
b. Matrix
c. Double counting
d. Coherent

35. A _____ of a curve is the envelope of a family of congruent circles centered on the curve. It generalises the concept of _____ lines.

It is sometimes called the offset curve but the term 'offset' often refers also to translation.

   a. Parallel
   b. Cycloid
   c. Bifolium
   d. Cissoid

36. The existence and properties of _____ are the basis of Euclid's parallel postulate. _____ are two lines on the same plane that do not intersect even assuming that lines extend to infinity in either direction.
   a. Square wheel
   b. Spidron
   c. Vertical translation
   d. Parallel lines

37. In mathematics, the _____ is an approach to finding a particular solution to certain inhomogeneous ordinary differential equations and recurrence relations. It is closely related to the annihilator method, but instead of using a particular kind of differential operator in order to find the best possible form of the particular solution, a 'guess' is made as to the appropriate form, which is then tested by differentiating the resulting equation. In this sense, the _____ is less formal but more intuitive than the annihilator method.
   a. Differential algebraic equations
   b. Linear differential equation
   c. Phase line
   d. Method of undetermined coefficients

38. In economics, business, retail, and accounting, a _____ is the value of money that has been used up to produce something, and hence is not available for use anymore. In business, the _____ may be one of acquisition, in which case the amount of money expended to acquire it is counted as _____. In this case, money is the input that is gone in order to acquire the thing.
   a. 2-3 heap
   b. 1-center problem
   c. 120-cell
   d. Cost

39. In economics, the cross elasticity of demand and _____ measures the responsiveness of the quantity demanded of a good to a change in the price of another good.

It is measured as the percentage change in quantity demanded for the first good that occurs in response to a percentage change in price of the second good. For example, if, in response to a 10% increase in the price of fuel, the quantity of new cars that are fuel inefficient demanded decreased by 20%, the cross elasticity of demand would be -20%/10% = -2.

a. Marginal rate of substitution
b. 1-center problem
c. Cross price elasticity of demand
d. Supply and demand

40. In mathematics a _____ is an inequality which involves a linear function.

When operating in terms of real numbers, linear inequalities are the ones written in the forms

$$f(x) < b \text{ or } f(x) \leq b,$$

where f(x) is a linear functional in real numbers and b is a constant real number. Alternatively, these may be viewed as

$$g(x) < 0 \text{ or } g(x) \leq 0,$$

where g(x) is an affine function.

a. Levi-Civita symbol
b. Generalized singular value decomposition
c. Linear inequality
d. Split-complex number

41. In mathematics, an _____ is a statement about the relative size or order of two objects, or about whether they are the same or not

- The notation a < b means that a is less than b.
- The notation a > b means that a is greater than b.
- The notation a ≠ b means that a is not equal to b, but does not say that one is bigger than the other or even that they can be compared in size.

In all these cases, a is not equal to b, hence, '_____'.

These relations are known as strict _____

- The notation a ≤ b means that a is less than or equal to b;
- The notation a ≥ b means that a is greater than or equal to b;

An additional use of the notation is to show that one quantity is much greater than another, normally by several orders of magnitude.

- The notation a << b means that a is much less than b.
- The notation a >> b means that a is much greater than b.

If the sense of the _____ is the same for all values of the variables for which its members are defined, then the _____ is called an 'absolute' or 'unconditional' _____. If the sense of an _____ holds only for certain values of the variables involved, but is reversed or destroyed for other values of the variables, it is called a conditional _____.

An _____ may appear unsolvable because it only states whether a number is larger or smaller than another number; but it is possible to apply the same operations for equalities to inequalities. For example, to find x for the _____ 10x > 23 one would divide 23 by 10.

a. A chemical equation
b. A Mathematical Theory of Communication
c. A posteriori
d. Inequality

42. In mathematics, _____ are used in the study of chance and probability. They were developed to assist in the analysis of games of chance, stochastic events, and the results of scientific experiments by capturing only the mathematical properties necessary to answer probabilistic questions. Further formalizations have firmly grounded the entity in the theoretical domains of mathematics by making use of measure theory.
a. Median polish
b. Statistical dispersion
c. Statistics
d. Random variables

43. In economics, specifically cost accounting, the _____ is the point at which cost or expenses and revenue are equal: there is no net loss or gain, and one has 'broken even'. Therefore has not made a profit or a loss.

Chapter 1. FUNCTIONS AND LINEAR MODELS

In the linear Cost-Volume-Profit Analysis model, the _____ can be directly computed in terms of Total Revenue and Total Costs as:

$$TR = TC$$
$$P \times X = TFC + V \times X$$
$$P \times X - V \times X = TFC$$
$$(P - V) \times X = TFC$$
$$X = \frac{TFC}{P - V}$$

where:

- TFC is Total Fixed Costs,
- P is Unit Sale Price, and
- V is Unit Variable Cost.

The _____ can alternatively be computed as the point where Contribution equals Fixed Costs.

The quantity $(P - V)$ is of interest in its own right, and is called the Unit Contribution Margin: it is the marginal profit per unit, or alternatively the portion of each sale that contributes to Fixed Costs. Thus the _____ can be more simply computed as the point where Total Contribution = Total Fixed Cost:

$$\text{Total Contribution} = \text{Total Fixed Costs}$$
$$\text{Unit Contribution} \times \text{Number of Units} = \text{Total Fixed Costs}$$
$$\text{Number of Units} = \frac{\text{Total Fixed Costs}}{\text{Unit Contribution}}$$

In currency units to reach break-even, one can use the above calculation and multiply by Price, or equivalently use the Contribution Margin Ratio to compute it as:

$$\text{Break-even(in Sales)} = \frac{\text{Fixed Costs}}{C/P}.$$

R=C Where R is revenue generated C is cost incurred.

a. 1-center problem
b. 120-cell
c. Small numbers game
d. Break-even point

Chapter 1. FUNCTIONS AND LINEAR MODELS

44. In microeconomics, _____ is the term used to refer to total when marginal cost is subtracted from marginal revenue. Under the marginal approach to profit maximization, to maximize profits, a firm should continue to produce a good until _____ is zero. Profit Maximization - The Marginal Approach

{{Economics-stub}}

.

   a. Marginal profit
   b. 1-center problem
   c. 2-3 heap
   d. 120-cell

45. In mathematics, a stochastic matrix, probability matrix, or _____ is used to describe the transitions of a Markov chain. It has found use in probability theory, statistics and linear algebra, as well as computer science. There are several different definitions and types of stochastic matrices;

> A right stochastic matrix is a square matrix each of whose rows consists of nonnegative real numbers, with each row summing to 1.

   a. Sylvester matrix
   b. Hessenberg matrix
   c. Pick matrix
   d. Transition matrix

46. In computational complexity theory, an algorithm is said to take _____ if the asymptotic upper bound for the time it requires is proportional to the size of the input, which is usually denoted n.

Informally spoken, the running time increases linearly with the size of the input. For example, a procedure that adds up all elements of a list requires time proportional to the length of the list.

   a. Time-constructible function
   b. Truth table reduction
   c. Constructible function
   d. Linear time

47. In optics, _____ is the phenomenon in which the phase velocity of a wave depends on its frequency. Media having such a property are termed dispersive media.

The most familiar example of _____ is probably a rainbow, in which _____ causes the spatial separation of a white light into components of different wavelengths.

a. Depth
b. Boussinesq approximation
c. Crib
d. Dispersion

48. Initial objects are also called _____, and terminal objects are also called final.
a. Colimit
b. Terminal object
c. Direct limit
d. Coterminal

49. _____ of an object is its speed in a particular direction.
a. Discontinuity
b. Rolle's Theorem
c. Maxima
d. Velocity

50. In complex analysis, the _____ is a complex number which describes the behavior of line integrals of a meromorphic function around a singularity. _____s can be computed quite easily and, once known, allow the determination of more complicated path integrals via the _____ theorem.

The _____ of a meromorphic function f at an isolated singularity a, often denoted Res is the unique value R such that $f(z) - \dfrac{R}{(z-a)}$ has an analytic antiderivative in a punctured disk $0 < |z - a| < \delta$.

a. Functional
b. Residue
c. Function
d. Block size

51. _____ is the likelihood or chance that something is the case or will happen. Theoretical _____ is used extensively in areas such as statistics, mathematics, science and philosophy to draw conclusions about the likelihood of potential events and the underlying mechanics of complex systems.

Chapter 1. FUNCTIONS AND LINEAR MODELS

The word _____ does not have a consistent direct definition.

a. Discrete random variable
b. Probability
c. Standardized moment
d. Statistical significance

52. The _____ Evaluation and Review Technique, commonly abbreviated PERT, is a model for project management designed to analyze and represent the tasks involved in completing a given project.

PERT is a method to analyze the involved tasks in completing a given project, especially the time needed to complete each task, and identifying the minimum time needed to complete the total project.

This model was invented by Booz Allen Hamilton, Inc.

a. Program
b. Key server
c. Battle of the Sexes
d. Huge

53. _____ is the addition of a set of numbers; the result is their sum or total. An interim or present total of a _____ process is termed the running total. The 'numbers' to be summed may be natural numbers, complex numbers, matrices, or still more complicated objects.

a. 120-cell
b. 2-3 heap
c. 1-center problem
d. Summation

54. In mathematics, a _____ is a constant multiplicative factor of a certain object. For example, in the expression $9x^2$, the _____ of x^2 is 9.

The object can be such things as a variable, a vector, a function, etc.

a. Fibonacci polynomials
b. Multivariate division algorithm
c. Coefficient
d. Stability radius

55. In probability theory and statistics, _____ indicates the strength and direction of a linear relationship between two random variables. That is in contrast with the usage of the term in colloquial speech, denoting any relationship, not necessarily linear. In general statistical usage, _____ or co-relation refers to the departure of two random variables from independence.
   a. Correlation
   b. Summary statistics
   c. Random variables
   d. Sample size

56. _____ is a general term used in explaining dependence on parameters, and implying the possibility of counting the number of those parameters. In mathematical terms, the _____ are the dimensions of a phase space.

In mechanics, for each particle belonging to a system, and for each independent direction in which movement is possible, two _____ are defined, one describing the particle's momentum in that direction, the other describing the particle's position along an axis defined by that direction.

   a. Degrees of freedom
   b. Character
   c. Decidable
   d. Battle of the Sexes

57. In mathematics, especially in set theory, a set A is a _____ of a set B if A is 'contained' inside B. Notice that A and B may coincide. The relationship of one set being a _____ of another is called inclusion.
   a. Cartesian product
   b. Horizontal line test
   c. Set of all sets
   d. Subset

Chapter 2. SYSTEMS OF LINEAR EQUATIONS AND MATRICES

1. A _____ is a software program that facilitates symbolic mathematics. The core functionality of a CAS is manipulation of mathematical expressions in symbolic form.

The symbolic manipulations supported typically include

- simplification to the smallest possible expression or some standard form, including automatic simplification with assumptions and simplification with constraints
- substitution of symbolic, functors or numeric values for expressions
- change of form of expressions: expanding products and powers, partial and full factorization, rewriting as partial fractions, constraint satisfaction, rewriting trigonometric functions as exponentials, etc.
- partial and total differentiation
- symbolic constrained and unconstrained global optimization
- solution of linear and some non-linear equations over various domains
- solution of some differential and difference equations
- taking some limits
- some indefinite and definite integration, including multidimensional integrals
- integral transforms
- arbitrary-precision numeric operations
- Series operations such as expansion, summation and products
- matrix operations including products, inverses, etc.
- display of mathematical expressions in two-dimensional mathematical form, often using typesetting systems similar to TeX
- add-ons for use in applied mathematics such as physics packages for physical computation
- plotting graphs and parametric plots of functions in two and three dimensions, and animating them
- APIs for linking it on an external program such as a database, or using in a programming language to use the _____
- drawing charts and diagrams
- string manipulation such as matching and searching
- statistical computation
- Theorem proving and verification
- graphic production and editing such as CGI and signal processing as image processing
- sound synthesis

Many also include a programming language, allowing users to implement their own algorithms.

Some _____s focus on a specific area of application; these are typically developed in academia and are free.

a. 2-3 heap
b. 120-cell
c. 1-center problem
d. Computer algebra system

Chapter 2. SYSTEMS OF LINEAR EQUATIONS AND MATRICES

2. A _____ is an algebraic equation in which each term is either a constant or the product of a constant and a single variable. _____s can have one, two, three or more variables.

_____s occur with great regularity in applied mathematics.

   a. Quartic equation
   b. Difference of two squares
   c. Quadratic equation
   d. Linear equation

3. In mathematics, a _____ is a constant multiplicative factor of a certain object. For example, in the expression $9x^2$, the _____ of x^2 is 9.

The object can be such things as a variable, a vector, a function, etc.

   a. Fibonacci polynomials
   b. Multivariate division algorithm
   c. Stability radius
   d. Coefficient

4. A _____ is a mathematical model of a system based on the use of a linear operator. _____s typically exhibit features and properties that are much simpler than the general, nonlinear case. As a mathematical abstraction or idealization, _____s find important applications in automatic control theory, signal processing, and telecommunications.

   a. Linear system
   b. Predispositioning Theory
   c. Percolation
   d. Hybrid system

5. In abstract algebra, a field extension L /K is called _____ if every element of L is _____ over K. Field extensions which are not _____.

For example, the field extension R/Q, that is the field of real numbers as an extension of the field of rational numbers, is transcendental, while the field extensions C/R and Q

a. Algebraic
b. Echo
c. Identity
d. Ideal

6. The solution of an algebraic equation, often one that seeks zeros of a polynomial, is sometimes said to admit an '_____' or a 'solution in radicals' if function that expresses the solution in terms of the coefficients relies only on addition, subtraction, multiplication, division, and the extraction of roots. The most well-known example is the solution

$$x = \frac{-b \pm \sqrt{b^2 - 4ac}}{2a}.$$

introduced in secondary school, of the quadratic equation

$$ax^2 + bx + c = 0$$

The Abel-Ruffini theorem states that the general quintic equation lacks an _____.

a. Algebraic function
b. Algebraic solution
c. Aperiodic finite-state automaton
d. Algebraic element

7. The mathematical concept of a _____ expresses the intuitive idea of deterministic dependence between two quantities, one of which is viewed as primary and the other as secondary. A _____ then is a way to associate a unique output for each input of a specified type, for example, a real number or an element of a given set.
a. Going up
b. Grill
c. Coherent
d. Function

8. In mathematics, an _____ is a statement about the relative size or order of two objects, or about whether they are the same or not

- The notation a < b means that a is less than b.
- The notation a > b means that a is greater than b.
- The notation a ≠ b means that a is not equal to b, but does not say that one is bigger than the other or even that they can be compared in size.

Chapter 2. SYSTEMS OF LINEAR EQUATIONS AND MATRICES

In all these cases, a is not equal to b, hence, '_____'.

These relations are known as strict _____

- The notation a ≤ b means that a is less than or equal to b;
- The notation a ≥ b means that a is greater than or equal to b;

An additional use of the notation is to show that one quantity is much greater than another, normally by several orders of magnitude.

- The notation a << b means that a is much less than b.
- The notation a >> b means that a is much greater than b.

If the sense of the _____ is the same for all values of the variables for which its members are defined, then the _____ is called an 'absolute' or 'unconditional' _____. If the sense of an _____ holds only for certain values of the variables involved, but is reversed or destroyed for other values of the variables, it is called a conditional _____.

An _____ may appear unsolvable because it only states whether a number is larger or smaller than another number; but it is possible to apply the same operations for equalities to inequalities. For example, to find x for the _____ 10x > 23 one would divide 23 by 10.

a. A chemical equation
b. A posteriori
c. A Mathematical Theory of Communication
d. Inequality

9. In mathematics a _____ is an inequality which involves a linear function.

When operating in terms of real numbers, linear inequalities are the ones written in the forms

$$f(x) < b \text{ or } f(x) \leq b,$$

where f(x) is a linear functional in real numbers and b is a constant real number. Alternatively, these may be viewed as

$$g(x) < 0 \text{ or } g(x) \leq 0,$$

where g(x) is an affine function.

Chapter 2. SYSTEMS OF LINEAR EQUATIONS AND MATRICES

a. Split-complex number
b. Levi-Civita symbol
c. Generalized singular value decomposition
d. Linear inequality

10. In mathematics, a _____ is a rectangular table of elements, which may be numbers or, more generally, any abstract quantities that can be added and multiplied. Matrices are used to describe linear equations, keep track of the coefficients of linear transformations and to record data that depend on multiple parameters. Matrices are described by the field of _____ theory.

   a. Compression
   b. Double counting
   c. Coherent
   d. Matrix

11. In linear algebra, the _____ of an n-by-n square matrix A is defined to be the sum of the elements on the main diagonal of A. wikimedia.org/math/8/2/b/82be32fa00bd97ebbc066aec3dfe72da.png">

where a_{ij} represents the entry on the ith row and jth column of A. Equivalently, the _____ of a matrix is the sum of its eigenvalues, making it an invariant with respect to a change of basis.

   a. Blinding
   b. Trace
   c. Constructivism
   d. Lattice

12. The _____ Evaluation and Review Technique, commonly abbreviated PERT, is a model for project management designed to analyze and represent the tasks involved in completing a given project.

PERT is a method to analyze the involved tasks in completing a given project, especially the time needed to complete each task, and identifying the minimum time needed to complete the total project.

This model was invented by Booz Allen Hamilton, Inc.

   a. Battle of the Sexes
   b. Huge
   c. Key server
   d. Program

Chapter 2. SYSTEMS OF LINEAR EQUATIONS AND MATRICES

13. In mathematics, a _____ is a collection of linear equations involving the same set of variables. For example,

$$3x + 2y - z = 1$$
$$2x - 2y + 4z = -2$$
$$-x + \tfrac{1}{2}y - z = 0$$

is a system of three equations in the three variables x, y, z. A solution to a linear system is an assignment of numbers to the variables such that all the equations are simultaneously satisfied.

a. Slutsky equation
b. Quintic equation
c. Hypsometric equation
d. System of linear equations

14. A _____ of a curve is the envelope of a family of congruent circles centered on the curve. It generalises the concept of _____ lines.

It is sometimes called the offset curve but the term 'offset' often refers also to translation.

a. Cycloid
b. Cissoid
c. Bifolium
d. Parallel

15. The existence and properties of _____ are the basis of Euclid's parallel postulate. _____ are two lines on the same plane that do not intersect even assuming that lines extend to infinity in either direction.
a. Vertical translation
b. Spidron
c. Parallel lines
d. Square wheel

16. In mathematics, the _____ is an approach to finding a particular solution to certain inhomogeneous ordinary differential equations and recurrence relations. It is closely related to the annihilator method, but instead of using a particular kind of differential operator in order to find the best possible form of the particular solution, a 'guess' is made as to the appropriate form, which is then tested by differentiating the resulting equation. In this sense, the _____ is less formal but more intuitive than the annihilator method.

Chapter 2. SYSTEMS OF LINEAR EQUATIONS AND MATRICES

a. Linear differential equation
b. Differential algebraic equations
c. Method of undetermined coefficients
d. Phase line

17. In logic, a theory is _____ if it does not contain a contradiction. The lack of contradiction can be defined in either semantic or syntactic terms. The semantic definition states that a theory is _____ if it has a model; this is the sense used in traditional Aristotelian logic, although in contemporary mathematical logic the term satisfiable is used instead.
    a. First-order logic
    b. Logic
    c. Second-order logic
    d. Consistent

18. In economics, specifically cost accounting, the _____ is the point at which cost or expenses and revenue are equal: there is no net loss or gain, and one has 'broken even'. Therefore has not made a profit or a loss.

In the linear Cost-Volume-Profit Analysis model, the _____ can be directly computed in terms of Total Revenue and Total Costs as:

$$TR = TC$$
$$P \times X = TFC + V \times X$$
$$P \times X - V \times X = TFC$$
$$(P - V) \times X = TFC$$
$$X = \frac{TFC}{P - V}$$

where:

- TFC is Total Fixed Costs,
- P is Unit Sale Price, and
- V is Unit Variable Cost.

The _____ can alternatively be computed as the point where Contribution equals Fixed Costs.

The quantity $(P - V)$ is of interest in its own right, and is called the Unit Contribution Margin: it is the marginal profit per unit, or alternatively the portion of each sale that contributes to Fixed Costs. Thus the _____ can be more simply computed as the point where Total Contribution = Total Fixed Cost:

$$\text{Total Contribution} = \text{Total Fixed Costs}$$
$$\text{Unit Contribution} \times \text{Number of Units} = \text{Total Fixed Costs}$$
$$\text{Number of Units} = \frac{\text{Total Fixed Costs}}{\text{Unit Contribution}}$$

In currency units to reach break-even, one can use the above calculation and multiply by Price, or equivalently use the Contribution Margin Ratio to compute it as:

$$\text{Break-even(in Sales)} = \frac{\text{Fixed Costs}}{C/P}.$$

R=C Where R is revenue generated C is cost incurred.

a. 120-cell
b. Break-even point
c. Small numbers game
d. 1-center problem

19. A _____ is an abstract model that uses mathematical language to describe the behavior of a system. Eykhoff defined a _____ as 'a representation of the essential aspects of an existing system which presents knowledge of that system in usable form'.

a. Total least squares
b. Mathematical model
c. Metaheuristic
d. Rata Die

20. In computational complexity theory, the complexity class _____ is the union of the classes in the exponential hierarchy.

$$\text{ELEMENTARY} = \text{EXP} \cup 2\text{EXP} \cup 3\text{EXP} \cup \cdots$$
$$= \text{DTIME}(2^n) \cup \text{DTIME}(2^{2^n}) \cup \text{DTIME}(2^{2^{2^n}}) \cup \cdots$$

The name was coined by Laszlo Kalmar, in the context of recursive functions and undecidability; most problems in it are far from _____. Some natural recursive problems lie outside _____, and are thus NONELEMENTARY.

a. A chemical equation
b. A posteriori
c. A Mathematical Theory of Communication
d. Elementary

21. In computer science an _____ is a data structure consisting of a group of elements that are accessed by indexing. In most programming languages each element has the same data type and the _____ occupies a contiguous area of storage.

Most programming languages have a built-in _____ data type, although what is called an _____ in the language documentation is sometimes really an associative _____.

a. Array
b. A Mathematical Theory of Communication
c. A chemical equation
d. A posteriori

22. _____ or amortisation is the process of decreasing an amount over a period of time. The word comes from Middle English amortisen to kill, alienate in mortmain, from Anglo-French amorteser, alteration of amortir, from Vulgar Latin admortire to kill, from Latin ad- + mort-, mors death. Particular instances of the term include:

- _____, the allocation of a lump sum amount to different time periods, particularly for loans and other forms of finance, including related interest or other finance charges.
    - _____ schedule, a table detailing each periodic payment on a loan, as generated by an _____ calculator.
    - Negative _____, an _____ schedule where the loan amount actually increases through not paying the full interest
- Amortized analysis, analyzing the execution cost of algorithms over a sequence of operations.
- _____ of capital expenditures of certain assets under accounting rules, particularly intangible assets, in a manner analogous to depreciation.
- _____

_____ is also used in the context of zoning regulations and describes the time in which a property owner has to relocate when the property's use constitutes a preexisting nonconforming use under zoning regulations.

- Depreciation

Chapter 2. SYSTEMS OF LINEAR EQUATIONS AND MATRICES

a. Amortization
b. Identity
c. Origin
d. ISAAC

23. An _____ is a table detailing each periodic payment on a amortizing loan, as generated by an amortization calculator.

While a portion of every payment is applied towards both the interest and the principal balance of the loan, the exact amount applied to principal each time varies. An _____ reveals the specific monetary amount put towards interest, as well as the specific put towards the Principal balance, with each payment.

a. Amortization schedule
b. Accounts receivable
c. A chemical equation
d. A Mathematical Theory of Communication

24. In mathematics, the _____ of a number n is the number that, when added to n, yields zero. The _____ of n is denoted −n. For example, 7 is −7, because 7 + (−7) = 0, and the _____ of −0.3 is 0.3, because −0.3 + 0.3 = 0.

a. Additive inverse
b. Arity
c. Associativity
d. Algebraic structure

25. In linear algebra, the _____ of a matrix is obtained by changing a matrix in some way.

Given the matrices A and B, where:

$$A = \begin{bmatrix} 1 & 3 & 2 \\ 2 & 0 & 1 \\ 5 & 2 & 2 \end{bmatrix}, \quad B = \begin{bmatrix} 4 \\ 3 \\ 1 \end{bmatrix}$$

Then, the _____ is written as:

$$(A|B) = \begin{bmatrix} 1 & 3 & 2 & 4 \\ 2 & 0 & 1 & 3 \\ 5 & 2 & 2 & 1 \end{bmatrix}$$

This is useful when solving systems of linear equations or the _____ may also be used to find the inverse of a matrix by combining it with the identity matrix.

Let C be a square 2×2 matrix where
$$C = \begin{bmatrix} 1 & 3 \\ -5 & 0 \end{bmatrix}$$

To find the inverse of C we create where I is the 2×2 identity matrix.

a. Alternating sign matrix
b. Augmented matrix
c. Eigendecomposition
d. Unimodular polynomial matrix

26. In linear algebra, _____ is a version of Gaussian elimination that puts zeros both above and below each pivot element as it goes from the top row of the given matrix to the bottom. In other words, _____ brings a matrix to reduced row echelon form, whereas Gaussian elimination takes it only as far as row echelon form. Every matrix has a reduced row echelon form, and this algorithm is guaranteed to produce it.
  a. Gauss-Jordan elimination
  b. Spheroidal wave functions
  c. Lax equivalence theorem
  d. Conservation form

27. In linear algebra a matrix is in row echelon form if

- All nonzero rows are above any rows of all zeroes, and
- The leading coefficient of a row is always strictly to the right of the leading coefficient of the row above it.

This is the definition used in this article, but some texts add a third condition:

- The leading coefficient of each nonzero row is one.

A matrix is in _____ (also called row canonical form) if it satisfies the above three conditions, and if, in addition

- Every leading coefficient is the only nonzero entry in its column.

The first non-zero entry in each row is called a pivot.

This matrix is in _____ :

$$\begin{bmatrix} 0 & 1 & 4 & 0 & 0 \\ 0 & 0 & 0 & 1 & 0 \\ 0 & 0 & 0 & 0 & 1 \\ 0 & 0 & 0 & 0 & 0 \end{bmatrix}.$$

The following matrix is also in row echelon form, but not in reduced row form:

$$\begin{bmatrix} 1 & 1 & 1 & 1 \\ 0 & 9 & 0 & 2 \\ 0 & 0 & 0 & 3 \end{bmatrix}.$$

However, this matrix is not in row echelon form, as the leading coefficient of row 3 is not strictly to the right of the leading coefficient of row 2.

$$\begin{bmatrix} 1 & 2 & 3 & 4 \\ 0 & 3 & 7 & 2 \\ 0 & 2 & 0 & 0 \end{bmatrix}$$

Every non-zero matrix can be reduced to an infinite number of echelon forms (they can all be multiples of each other, for example) via elementary matrix transformations.

a. Reduced row echelon form
b. Folded spectrum method
c. Basic Linear Algebra Subprograms
d. Pseudospectrum

28. In linear algebra a matrix is in _____ if

- All nonzero rows are above any rows of all zeroes, and
- The leading coefficient of a row is always strictly to the right of the leading coefficient of the row above it.

This is the definition used in this article, but some texts add a third condition:

- The leading coefficient of each nonzero row is one.

Chapter 2. SYSTEMS OF LINEAR EQUATIONS AND MATRICES

A matrix is in reduced _____ if it satisfies the above three conditions, and if, in addition

- Every leading coefficient is the only nonzero entry in its column.

The first non-zero entry in each row is called a pivot.

This matrix is in reduced _____:

$$\begin{bmatrix} 0 & 1 & 4 & 0 & 0 \\ 0 & 0 & 0 & 1 & 0 \\ 0 & 0 & 0 & 0 & 1 \\ 0 & 0 & 0 & 0 & 0 \end{bmatrix}.$$

The following matrix is also in _____, but not in reduced row form:

$$\begin{bmatrix} 1 & 1 & 1 & 1 \\ 0 & 9 & 0 & 2 \\ 0 & 0 & 0 & 3 \end{bmatrix}.$$

However, this matrix is not in _____, as the leading coefficient of row 3 is not strictly to the right of the leading coefficient of row 2.

$$\begin{bmatrix} 1 & 2 & 3 & 4 \\ 0 & 3 & 7 & 2 \\ 0 & 2 & 0 & 0 \end{bmatrix}$$

Every non-zero matrix can be reduced to an infinite number of echelon forms via elementary matrix transformations.

a. Row echelon form
b. Reduced row echelon form
c. Portable, Extensible Toolkit for Scientific Computation
d. Gaussian elimination

29. In mathematics, _____ and undefined are used to explain whether or not expressions have meaningful, sensible, and unambiguous values. Not all branches of mathematics come to the same conclusion.

The following expressions are undefined in all contexts, but remarks in the analysis section may apply.

a. LHS
b. Toy model
c. Plugging in
d. Defined

30. In statistics, given a sample $(Y_i, X_{i1}, \ldots, X_{ip})$, $i = 1, \ldots, n$ the most general form of _____ is formulated as

$$Y_i = \beta_0 + \beta_1 \phi_1(X_{i1}) + \ldots + \beta_p \phi_p(X_{ip}) + \varepsilon_i \qquad i = 1, \ldots, n$$

where $\phi_1, \ldots, \phi_p$ may be nonlinear functions.

In matrix notation this model can be written as

$$Y = X\beta + \varepsilon$$

where Y is an n × 1 column vector, X is an n × matrix, β is a × 1 vector of parameters, and ε is an n × 1 vector of errors, which are uncorrelated random variables each with expected value 0 and variance σ^2. Note that depending on the context the sample can be seen as fixed, or random.

a. Risk measure
b. Linear model
c. Life table
d. Risk aversion

31. In mathematics, the _____ is a conic section, the intersection of a right circular conical surface and a plane parallel to a generating straight line of that surface. Given a point and a line that lie in a plane, the locus of points in that plane that are equidistant to them is a _____.

A particular case arises when the plane is tangent to the conical surface of a circle.

a. Parabola
b. Directrix
c. Dandelin sphere
d. Matrix representation of conic sections

Chapter 2. SYSTEMS OF LINEAR EQUATIONS AND MATRICES

32. In ecology, predation describes a biological interaction where a _____ (an organism that is hunting) feeds on its prey, the organism that is attacked. _____s may or may not kill their prey prior to feeding on them, but the act of predation always results in the death of the prey. The other main category of consumption is detritivory, the consumption of dead organic material (detritus.)
    a. 1-center problem
    b. 120-cell
    c. Prey
    d. Predator

33. In mathematics, the _____ is a direct product of sets. The _____ is named after René Descartes, whose formulation of analytic geometry gave rise to this concept.

Specifically, the _____ of two sets X and Y, denoted X × Y, is the set of all possible ordered pairs whose first component is a member of X and whose second component is a member of Y:

$$X \times Y = \{(x,y) | x \in X \text{ and } y \in Y\}.$$

For example, the _____ of the 13-element set of standard playing card ranks {Ace, King, Queen, Jack, 10, 9, 8, 7, 6, 5, 4, 3, 2} and the four-element set of card suits {â™ , â™¥, â™¦, â™£} is the 52-element set of all possible playing cards ,, ...,,, ...,,}.

   a. Set of all sets
   b. Choice function
   c. Disjoint sets
   d. Cartesian product

34. A _____ typically refers to a class of handheld calculators that are capable of plotting graphs, solving simultaneous equations, and performing numerous other tasks with variables. Most popular _____s are also programmable, allowing the user to create customized programs, typically for scientific/engineering and education applications. Due to their large displays intended for graphing, they can also accommodate several lines of text and calculations at a time.
    a. Bump mapping
    b. Genus
    c. Support vector machines
    d. Graphing calculator

35. A _____ is a device for performing mathematical calculations, distinguished from a computer by having a limited problem solving ability and an interface optimized for interactive calculation rather than programming. _____s can be hardware or software, and mechanical or electronic, and are often built into devices such as PDAs or mobile phones.

Modern electronic _____s are generally small, digital, and usually inexpensive.

a. 2-3 heap
b. 1-center problem
c. Calculator
d. 120-cell

Chapter 3. MATRIX ALGEBRA AND APPLICATIONS

1. A _____ is an abstract model that uses mathematical language to describe the behavior of a system. Eykhoff defined a _____ as 'a representation of the essential aspects of an existing system which presents knowledge of that system in usable form'.
   a. Total least squares
   b. Mathematical model
   c. Rata Die
   d. Metaheuristic

2. In mathematics, _____ and undefined are used to explain whether or not expressions have meaningful, sensible, and unambiguous values. Not all branches of mathematics come to the same conclusion.

The following expressions are undefined in all contexts, but remarks in the analysis section may apply.

   a. Toy model
   b. Defined
   c. LHS
   d. Plugging in

3. In mathematics, a _____ is a rectangular table of elements, which may be numbers or, more generally, any abstract quantities that can be added and multiplied. Matrices are used to describe linear equations, keep track of the coefficients of linear transformations and to record data that depend on multiple parameters. Matrices are described by the field of _____ theory.
   a. Double counting
   b. Compression
   c. Coherent
   d. Matrix

4. A _____ typically refers to a class of handheld calculators that are capable of plotting graphs, solving simultaneous equations, and performing numerous other tasks with variables. Most popular _____s are also programmable, allowing the user to create customized programs, typically for scientific/engineering and education applications. Due to their large displays intended for graphing, they can also accommodate several lines of text and calculations at a time.
   a. Genus
   b. Bump mapping
   c. Support vector machines
   d. Graphing calculator

5. _____ or amortisation is the process of decreasing an amount over a period of time. The word comes from Middle English amortisen to kill, alienate in mortmain, from Anglo-French amorteser, alteration of amortir, from Vulgar Latin admortire to kill, from Latin ad- + mort-, mors death. Particular instances of the term include:

- _____, the allocation of a lump sum amount to different time periods, particularly for loans and other forms of finance, including related interest or other finance charges.
    - _____ schedule, a table detailing each periodic payment on a loan, as generated by an _____ calculator.
    - Negative _____, an _____ schedule where the loan amount actually increases through not paying the full interest
- Amortized analysis, analyzing the execution cost of algorithms over a sequence of operations.
- _____ of capital expenditures of certain assets under accounting rules, particularly intangible assets, in a manner analogous to depreciation.
- _____

_____ is also used in the context of zoning regulations and describes the time in which a property owner has to relocate when the property's use constitutes a preexisting nonconforming use under zoning regulations.

- Depreciation

a. Amortization
b. Identity
c. Origin
d. ISAAC

6. An _____ is a table detailing each periodic payment on a amortizing loan, as generated by an amortization calculator.

While a portion of every payment is applied towards both the interest and the principal balance of the loan, the exact amount applied to principal each time varies. An _____ reveals the specific monetary amount put towards interest, as well as the specific put towards the Principal balance, with each payment.

a. Amortization schedule
b. A chemical equation
c. Accounts receivable
d. A Mathematical Theory of Communication

7. A _____ is a device for performing mathematical calculations, distinguished from a computer by having a limited problem solving ability and an interface optimized for interactive calculation rather than programming. _____s can be hardware or software, and mechanical or electronic, and are often built into devices such as PDAs or mobile phones.

Modern electronic _____s are generally small, digital, and usually inexpensive.

   a. 2-3 heap
   b. 1-center problem
   c. Calculator
   d. 120-cell

8. In linear algebra, a row vector or _____ is a 1 × n matrix, that is, a matrix consisting of a single row:

$$\mathbf{x} = \begin{bmatrix} x_1 & x_2 & \cdots & x_m \end{bmatrix}.$$

The transpose of a row vector is a column vector:

$$\begin{bmatrix} x_1 \\ x_2 \\ \vdots \\ x_m \end{bmatrix} = \begin{bmatrix} x_1 & x_2 & \cdots & x_m \end{bmatrix}^{\mathrm{T}}.$$

The set of all row vectors forms a vector space which is the dual space to the set of all column vectors.

Row vectors are sometimes written using the following non-standard notation:

$$\mathbf{x} = \begin{bmatrix} x_1, x_2, \ldots, x_m \end{bmatrix}.$$

- Matrix multiplication involves the action of multiplying each row vector of one matrix by each column vector of another matrix.

- The dot product of two vectors a and b is equivalent to multiplying the row vector representation of a by the column vector representation of b:

$$\mathbf{a} \cdot \mathbf{b} = \begin{bmatrix} a_1 & a_2 & a_3 \end{bmatrix} \begin{bmatrix} b_1 \\ b_2 \\ b_3 \end{bmatrix}.$$

a. Woodbury matrix identity
b. Dual vector space
c. Gram-Schmidt process
d. Row matrix

9. In mathematics, an _____ is a statement about the relative size or order of two objects, or about whether they are the same or not

- The notation a < b means that a is less than b.
- The notation a > b means that a is greater than b.
- The notation a ≠ b means that a is not equal to b, but does not say that one is bigger than the other or even that they can be compared in size.

In all these cases, a is not equal to b, hence, '_____'.

These relations are known as strict _____

- The notation a ≤ b means that a is less than or equal to b;
- The notation a ≥ b means that a is greater than or equal to b;

An additional use of the notation is to show that one quantity is much greater than another, normally by several orders of magnitude.

- The notation a << b means that a is much less than b.
- The notation a >> b means that a is much greater than b.

If the sense of the _____ is the same for all values of the variables for which its members are defined, then the _____ is called an 'absolute' or 'unconditional' _____. If the sense of an _____ holds only for certain values of the variables involved, but is reversed or destroyed for other values of the variables, it is called a conditional _____.

An _____ may appear unsolvable because it only states whether a number is larger or smaller than another number; but it is possible to apply the same operations for equalities to inequalities. For example, to find x for the _____ 10x > 23 one would divide 23 by 10.

a. A Mathematical Theory of Communication
b. A chemical equation
c. A posteriori
d. Inequality

Chapter 3. MATRIX ALGEBRA AND APPLICATIONS

10. _____ is a branch of mathematics which focuses on the study of matrices. Initially a sub-branch of linear algebra, it has grown to cover subjects related to graph theory, algebra, combinatorics, and statistics as well.

The term matrix was first coined in 1848 by J.J. Sylvester as a name of an array of numbers.

   a. Semi-simple operators
   b. Pairing
   c. Segre classification
   d. Matrix theory

11. In physics and in _____ calculus, a _____ is a concept characterized by a magnitude and a direction. A _____ can be thought of as an arrow in Euclidean space, drawn from an initial point A pointing to a terminal point B.
   a. Deviation
   b. Constraint
   c. Dominance
   d. Vector

12. In computer science an _____ is a data structure consisting of a group of elements that are accessed by indexing. In most programming languages each element has the same data type and the _____ occupies a contiguous area of storage.

Most programming languages have a built-in _____ data type, although what is called an _____ in the language documentation is sometimes really an associative _____.

   a. A posteriori
   b. A Mathematical Theory of Communication
   c. A chemical equation
   d. Array

13. _____ is the mathematical operation of scaling one number by another. It is one of the four basic operations in elementary arithmetic.

_____ is defined for whole numbers in terms of repeated addition; for example, 4 multiplied by 3 can be calculated by adding 3 copies of 4 together:

$$4 + 4 + 4 = 12.$$

_____ of rational numbers and real numbers is defined by systematic generalization of this basic idea.

a. Least common multiple
b. The number 0 is even.
c. Highest common factor
d. Multiplication

14. In mathematics, _____ is one of the basic operations defining a vector space in linear algebra. Note that _____ is different from scalar product which is an inner product between two vectors.

More specifically, if K is a field and V is a vector space over K, then _____ is a function from K × V to V.

a. Jordan normal form
b. Frobenius normal form
c. Non-negative matrix factorization
d. Scalar multiplication

15. In mathematics the _____ of a set which is equipped with the operation of addition is an element which, when added to any element x in the set, yields x. One of the most familiar additive identities is the number 0 from elementary mathematics, but additive identities occur in other mathematical structures where addition is defined, such as in groups and rings.

- The _____ familiar from elementary mathematics is zero, denoted 0. For example,

  5 + 0 = 5 = 0 + 5.

- In the natural numbers N and all of its supersets, the _____ is 0. Thus for any one of these numbers n,

  n + 0 = n = 0 + n.

Let N be a set which is closed under the operation of addition, denoted +. An _____ for N is any element e such that for any element n in N,

  e + n = n = n + e.

a. Unique factorization domain
b. Algebraically independent
c. Unit ring
d. Additive identity

16. In mathematics, the _____ of a number n is the number that, when added to n, yields zero. The _____ of n is denoted −n. For example, 7 is −7, because 7 + (−7) = 0, and the _____ of −0.3 is 0.3, because −0.3 + 0.3 = 0.
   a. Additive inverse
   b. Algebraic structure
   c. Arity
   d. Associativity

17. In mathematics, _____ is a property that a binary operation can have. It means that, within an expression containing two or more of the same associative operators in a row, the order that the operations are performed does not matter as long as the sequence of the operands is not changed. That is, rearranging the parentheses in such an expression will not change its value.
   a. Idempotence
   b. Associativity
   c. Algebraically closed
   d. Unital

18. The _____ is a rule which states that when you add or multiply numbers, changing the order doesn't change the result.
   a. Semigroupoid
   b. Commutative law
   c. Coimage
   d. Conditional event algebra

19. In mathematics, and in particular in abstract algebra, distributivity is a property of binary operations that generalises the _____ law from elementary algebra.
   a. General linear group
   b. Distributive
   c. Closure with a twist
   d. Permutation

20. In mathematics, the term _____ has several different important meanings:

- An _____ is an equality that remains true regardless of the values of any variables that appear within it, to distinguish it from an equality which is true under more particular conditions. For this, the 'triple bar' symbol ≡ is sometimes used.
- In algebra, an _____ or _____ element of a set S with a binary operation Â· is an element e that, when combined with any element x of S, produces that same x. That is, eÂ·x = xÂ·e = x for all x in S.
    - The _____ function from a set S to itself, often denoted id or id_S, s the function such that i = x for all x in S. This function serves as the _____ element in the set of all functions from S to itself with respect to function composition.
    - In linear algebra, the _____ matrix of size n is the n-by-n square matrix with ones on the main diagonal and zeros elsewhere. This matrix serves as the _____ with respect to matrix multiplication.

A common example of the first meaning is the trigonometric _____

$$\sin^2 \theta + \cos^2 \theta = 1$$

which is true for all real values of θ, as opposed to

$$\cos \theta = 1,$$

which is true only for some values of θ, not all. For example, the latter equation is true when $\theta = 0$, false when $\theta = 2$

The concepts of 'additive _____' and 'multiplicative _____' are central to the Peano axioms. The number 0 is the 'additive _____' for integers, real numbers, and complex numbers. For the real numbers, for all $a \in \mathbb{R}$,

$$0 + a = a,$$

$$a + 0 = a, \text{ and}$$

$$0 + 0 = 0.$$

Similarly, The number 1 is the 'multiplicative _____' for integers, real numbers, and complex numbers.

a. Intersection
b. ARIA
c. Action
d. Identity

Chapter 3. MATRIX ALGEBRA AND APPLICATIONS

21. In informal language, a _____ is a function that swaps two elements of a set. More formally, given a finite set $X = \{a_1, a_2, \ldots, a_n\}$, a _____ is a permutation f, such that there exist indices i,j such that fj, fi and fk for all other indices k. This is often denoted as

For example, if X = {a,b,c,d,e}, the function σ given by

$$\sigma(a) = a$$
$$\sigma(b) = e$$
$$\sigma(c) = c$$
$$\sigma(d) = d$$
$$\sigma(e) = b$$

is a _____.

Any permutation can be expressed as the composition of _____s.

a. C-35
b. Transposition
c. Bounded
d. Chiral

22. In mathematics, specifically in combinatorial commutative algebra, a convex lattice polytope P is called _____ if it has the following property: given any positive integer n, every lattice point of the dilation nP, obtained from P by scaling its vertices by the factor n and taking the convex hull of the resulting points, can be written as the sum of exactly n lattice points in P. This property plays an important role in the theory of toric varieties, where it corresponds to projective normality of the toric variety determined by P.

The simplex in R^k with the vertices at the origin and along the unit coordinate vectors is _____.

a. Hypercube
b. Demihypercubes
c. Polytetrahedron
d. Normal

23. The _____ is an important family of continuous probability distributions, applicable in many fields. Each member of the family may be defined by two parameters, location and scale: the mean and variance respectively. The standard _____ is the _____ with a mean of zero and a variance of one.

a. Normal distribution
b. Coefficient of variation
c. Null hypothesis
d. Percentile rank

24. In linear algebra, a _____ is a square matrix, A, that is equal to its transpose

$$A = A^T.$$

The entries of a _____ are symmetric with respect to the main diagonal. So if the entries are written as A =, then

$$a_{ij} = a_{ji}$$

for all indices i and j. The following 3×3 matrix is symmetric:

$$\begin{bmatrix} 1 & 2 & 3 \\ 2 & 4 & -5 \\ 3 & -5 & 6 \end{bmatrix}.$$

A matrix is called skew-symmetric or antisymmetric if its transpose is the same as its negative.

a. Conway triangle notation
b. Broken-line graph
c. Contour integration
d. Symmetric matrix

25. In differential geometry, a discipline within mathematics, a _____ is a subset of the tangent bundle of a manifold satisfying certain properties. _____s are used to build up notions of integrability, and specifically of a foliation of a manifold

a. Coherence
b. Discontinuity
c. Constraint
d. Distribution

26. In mathematics, a _____ is a constant multiplicative factor of a certain object. For example, in the expression $9x^2$, the _____ of x^2 is 9.

Chapter 3. MATRIX ALGEBRA AND APPLICATIONS 45

The object can be such things as a variable, a vector, a function, etc.

a. Fibonacci polynomials
b. Multivariate division algorithm
c. Stability radius
d. Coefficient

27. A _____ is an algebraic equation in which each term is either a constant or the product of a constant and a single variable. _____s can have one, two, three or more variables.

_____s occur with great regularity in applied mathematics.

a. Quartic equation
b. Quadratic equation
c. Linear equation
d. Difference of two squares

28. The mathematical concept of a _____ expresses the intuitive idea of deterministic dependence between two quantities, one of which is viewed as primary and the other as secondary. A _____ then is a way to associate a unique output for each input of a specified type, for example, a real number or an element of a given set.
a. Going up
b. Grill
c. Function
d. Coherent

29. In linear algebra, the _____ or unit matrix of size n is the n-by-n square matrix with ones on the main diagonal and zeros elsewhere. It is denoted by I_n, or simply by I if the size is immaterial or can be trivially determined by the context. (In some fields, such as quantum mechanics, the _____ is denoted by a boldface one, 1; otherwise it is identical to I.)
a. Associativity
b. Unital
c. Arity
d. Identity matrix

30. A _____ is a software program that facilitates symbolic mathematics. The core functionality of a CAS is manipulation of mathematical expressions in symbolic form.

Chapter 3. MATRIX ALGEBRA AND APPLICATIONS

The symbolic manipulations supported typically include

- simplification to the smallest possible expression or some standard form, including automatic simplification with assumptions and simplification with constraints
- substitution of symbolic, functors or numeric values for expressions
- change of form of expressions: expanding products and powers, partial and full factorization, rewriting as partial fractions, constraint satisfaction, rewriting trigonometric functions as exponentials, etc.
- partial and total differentiation
- symbolic constrained and unconstrained global optimization
- solution of linear and some non-linear equations over various domains
- solution of some differential and difference equations
- taking some limits
- some indefinite and definite integration, including multidimensional integrals
- integral transforms
- arbitrary-precision numeric operations
- Series operations such as expansion, summation and products
- matrix operations including products, inverses, etc.
- display of mathematical expressions in two-dimensional mathematical form, often using typesetting systems similar to TeX
- add-ons for use in applied mathematics such as physics packages for physical computation
- plotting graphs and parametric plots of functions in two and three dimensions, and animating them
- APIs for linking it on an external program such as a database, or using in a programming language to use the _____
- drawing charts and diagrams
- string manipulation such as matching and searching
- statistical computation
- Theorem proving and verification
- graphic production and editing such as CGI and signal processing as image processing
- sound synthesis

Many also include a programming language, allowing users to implement their own algorithms.

Some _____ s focus on a specific area of application; these are typically developed in academia and are free.

a. Computer algebra system
b. 2-3 heap
c. 1-center problem
d. 120-cell

Chapter 3. MATRIX ALGEBRA AND APPLICATIONS

31. A _____ is a mathematical model of a system based on the use of a linear operator. _____s typically exhibit features and properties that are much simpler than the general, nonlinear case. As a mathematical abstraction or idealization, _____s find important applications in automatic control theory, signal processing, and telecommunications.
   a. Hybrid system
   b. Percolation
   c. Linear system
   d. Predispositioning Theory

32. In linear algebra, the _____ of a matrix is obtained by changing a matrix in some way.

Given the matrices A and B, where:

$$A = \begin{bmatrix} 1 & 3 & 2 \\ 2 & 0 & 1 \\ 5 & 2 & 2 \end{bmatrix}, \quad B = \begin{bmatrix} 4 \\ 3 \\ 1 \end{bmatrix}$$

Then, the _____ is written as:

$$(A|B) = \begin{bmatrix} 1 & 3 & 2 & 4 \\ 2 & 0 & 1 & 3 \\ 5 & 2 & 2 & 1 \end{bmatrix}$$

This is useful when solving systems of linear equations or the _____ may also be used to find the inverse of a matrix by combining it with the identity matrix.

Let C be a square 2×2 matrix where
$$C = \begin{bmatrix} 1 & 3 \\ -5 & 0 \end{bmatrix}$$

To find the inverse of C we create where I is the 2×2 identity matrix.

   a. Unimodular polynomial matrix
   b. Alternating sign matrix
   c. Augmented matrix
   d. Eigendecomposition

33. In mathematics, a _____ is a set of real numbers with the property that any number that lies between two numbers in the set is also included in the set. For example, the set of all numbers x satisfying $0 \leq x \leq 1$ is an _____ which contains 0 and 1, as well as all numbers between them. Other examples of _____s are the set of all real numbers $\mathbb{R}$, the set of all positive real numbers, and the empty set.
   a. Order
   b. Annihilator
   c. Interval
   d. Ideal

34. In computational complexity theory, the complexity class _____ is the union of the classes in the exponential hierarchy.

$$\text{ELEMENTARY} = \text{EXP} \cup \text{2EXP} \cup \text{3EXP} \cup \cdots$$
$$= \text{DTIME}(2^n) \cup \text{DTIME}(2^{2^n}) \cup \text{DTIME}(2^{2^{2^n}}) \cup \cdots$$

The name was coined by Laszlo Kalmar, in the context of recursive functions and undecidability; most problems in it are far from _____. Some natural recursive problems lie outside _____, and are thus NONELEMENTARY.

   a. A chemical equation
   b. Elementary
   c. A Mathematical Theory of Communication
   d. A posteriori

35. In algebra, a _____ is a function depending on n that associates a scalar, de, to every n×n square matrix A. The fundamental geometric meaning of a _____ is as the scale factor for measure when A is regarded as a linear transformation. _____s are important both in calculus, where they enter the substitution rule for several variables, and in multilinear algebra.
   a. 1-center problem
   b. Pfaffian
   c. Determinant
   d. Functional determinant

36. In economics, an externality is an impact on any party not directly involved in an economic decision. An externality occurs when an economic activity causes _____ costs or _____ benefits to third party stakeholders who did not directly affect the economic transaction. Another term that often replaces externality is spillover.

a. External
b. A Mathematical Theory of Communication
c. A chemical equation
d. A posteriori

37. In linear algebra, a _____ is a square matrix in which the entries outside the main diagonal are all zero. The diagonal entries themselves may or may not be zero. Thus, the matrix D = with n columns and n rows is diagonal if:

$$d_{i,j} = 0 \text{ if } i \neq j \qquad \forall i,j \in \{1, 2, \ldots, n\}$$

For example, the following matrix is diagonal:

$$\begin{bmatrix} 1 & 0 & 0 \\ 0 & 4 & 0 \\ 0 & 0 & -3 \end{bmatrix}.$$

The term _____ may sometimes refer to a rectangular _____, which is an m-by-n matrix with only the entries of the form $d_{i,i}$ possibly non-zero; for example,

$$\begin{bmatrix} 1 & 0 & 0 \\ 0 & 4 & 0 \\ 0 & 0 & -3 \\ 0 & 0 & 0 \end{bmatrix}, \text{ or } \begin{bmatrix} 1 & 0 & 0 & 0 & 0 \\ 0 & 4 & 0 & 0 & 0 \\ 0 & 0 & -3 & 0 & 0 \end{bmatrix}.$$

a. Design matrix
b. Hankel matrix
c. Transition matrix
d. Diagonal matrix

38. In ecology, predation describes a biological interaction where a _____ (an organism that is hunting) feeds on its prey, the organism that is attacked. _____s may or may not kill their prey prior to feeding on them, but the act of predation always results in the death of the prey. The other main category of consumption is detritivory, the consumption of dead organic material (detritus.)

a. Prey
b. 1-center problem
c. 120-cell
d. Predator

Chapter 4. LINEAR PROGRAMMING

1. In mathematics, _____ is a technique for optimization of a linear objective function, subject to linear equality and linear inequality constraints. Informally, _____ determines the way to achieve the best outcome in a given mathematical model given some list of requirements represented as linear equations.

More formally, given a polytope, and a real-valued affine function

$$f(x_1, x_2, \ldots, x_n) = c_1 x_1 + c_2 x_2 + \cdots + c_n x_n + d$$

defined on this polytope, a _____ method will find a point in the polytope where this function has the smallest value.

   a. Linear programming relaxation
   b. Lin-Kernighan
   c. Descent direction
   d. Linear programming

2. In geometry, a _____ or n-_____ is an n-dimensional analogue of a triangle. Specifically, a _____ is the convex hull of a set of affinely independent points in some Euclidean space of dimension n or higher.

For example, a 0-_____ is a point, a 1-_____ is a line segment, a 2-_____ is a triangle, a 3-_____ is a tetrahedron, and a 4-_____ is a pentachoron.

   a. Hypercell
   b. Simplex
   c. Demihypercubes
   d. Polytetrahedron

3. In mathematical optimization theory, the simplex algorithm, created by the American mathematician George Dantzig in 1947, is a popular algorithm for numerical solution of the linear programming problem. The journal Computing in Science and Engineering listed it as one of the top 10 algorithms of the century.

An unrelated, but similarly named method is the Nelder-Mead method or downhill _____ due to Nelder ' Mead and is a numerical method for optimising many-dimensional unconstrained problems, belonging to the more general class of search algorithms.

   a. Differential evolution
   b. Fibonacci search
   c. Hill climbing
   d. Simplex method

4. _____ is an important tool for manufacturing and engineering, where it can have a major impact on the productivity of a process. In manufacturing, the purpose of _____ is to minimize the production time and costs, by telling a production facility what to make, when, with which staff, and on which equipment. Production _____ aims to maximize the efficiency of the operation and reduce costs.

   a. Critical point
   b. Boolean algebra
   c. Crib
   d. Scheduling

5. In mathematics, a _____ is a condition that a solution to an optimization problem must satisfy. There are two types of _____s: equality _____s and inequality _____s. The set of solutions that satisfy all _____s is called the feasible set.

   a. Decidable
   b. Concurrent
   c. Constraint
   d. Foci

6. In mathematics, an _____ is a statement about the relative size or order of two objects, or about whether they are the same or not

   - The notation a < b means that a is less than b.
   - The notation a > b means that a is greater than b.
   - The notation a ≠ b means that a is not equal to b, but does not say that one is bigger than the other or even that they can be compared in size.

In all these cases, a is not equal to b, hence, '_____'.

These relations are known as strict _____

   - The notation a ≤ b means that a is less than or equal to b;
   - The notation a ≥ b means that a is greater than or equal to b;

An additional use of the notation is to show that one quantity is much greater than another, normally by several orders of magnitude.

   - The notation a << b means that a is much less than b.
   - The notation a >> b means that a is much greater than b.

Chapter 4. LINEAR PROGRAMMING

If the sense of the _____ is the same for all values of the variables for which its members are defined, then the _____ is called an 'absolute' or 'unconditional' _____. If the sense of an _____ holds only for certain values of the variables involved, but is reversed or destroyed for other values of the variables, it is called a conditional _____.

An _____ may appear unsolvable because it only states whether a number is larger or smaller than another number; but it is possible to apply the same operations for equalities to inequalities. For example, to find x for the _____ 10x > 23 one would divide 23 by 10.

a. A chemical equation
b. A Mathematical Theory of Communication
c. A posteriori
d. Inequality

7. _____ methods are common techniques to compute the equilibrium configuration of molecules. The basic idea is that a stable state of a molecular system should correspond to a local minimum of their potential energy. This kind of calculation generally starts from an arbitrary state of molecules, then the mathematical procedure of optimization allows us to move atoms in a way to reduce the net forces to nearly zero.
a. A Mathematical Theory of Communication
b. A posteriori
c. Energy minimization
d. A chemical equation

8. In mathematics and computer science, an _____ is the problem of finding the best solution from all feasible solutions. More formally, an _____ A is a quadruple , where

- I is a set of instances;
- given an instance $x \in I$, f is the set of feasible solutions;
- given an instance x and a feasible solution y of x, m denotes the measure of y, which is usually a positive real.
- g is the goal function, and is either min or max.

The goal is then to find for some instance x an optimal solution, that is, a feasible solution y with

$$m(x, y) = g\{m(x, y') \mid y' \in f(x)\}.$$

For each _____, there is a corresponding decision problem that asks whether there is a feasible solution for some particular measure m_0. For example, if there is a graph G which contains vertices u and v, an _____ might be 'find a path from u to v that uses the fewest edges'. This problem might have an answer of, say, 4.

a. Optimization problem
b. Interactive proof system
c. Element uniqueness
d. Approximation algorithms

9. In mathematics, computing, linguistics and related subjects, an _____ is a sequence of finite instructions, often used for calculation and data processing. It is formally a type of effective method in which a list of well-defined instructions for completing a task will, when given an initial state, proceed through a well-defined series of successive states, eventually terminating in an end-state. The transition from one state to the next is not necessarily deterministic; some _____s, known as probabilistic _____s, incorporate randomness.

a. Approximate counting algorithm
b. In-place algorithm
c. Out-of-core
d. Algorithm

10. In mathematics, an inequality is a statement about the relative size or order of two objects. For example 14 > 10, or 14 is _____ 10. The notation a > b means that a is _____ b and 'a' would be to the right of 'b' on a number line.

a. Greater than
b. Cauchy-Schwarz inequality
c. FKG inequality
d. Minkowski inequality

11. _____ is the mathematical operation of scaling one number by another. It is one of the four basic operations in elementary arithmetic.

_____ is defined for whole numbers in terms of repeated addition; for example, 4 multiplied by 3 can be calculated by adding 3 copies of 4 together:

$$4 + 4 + 4 = 12.$$

_____ of rational numbers and real numbers is defined by systematic generalization of this basic idea.

a. The number 0 is even.
b. Least common multiple
c. Highest common factor
d. Multiplication

Chapter 4. LINEAR PROGRAMMING

12. In mathematical writing, the adjective _____ is used to modify technical terms which have multiple meanings. It indicates that the exclusive meaning of the term is to be understood. (More formally, one could say that this is the meaning which implies the other meanings.)

   a. Well-behaved
   b. Jargon
   c. Percentage points
   d. Strict

13. _____ is either of the two parts into which a plane divides the three-dimensional space. More generally, a _____ is either of the two parts into which a hyperplane divides an affine space.

   a. Half-space
   b. Simple polytope
   c. Parallelogram law
   d. Pendent

14. In mathematics, a _____ is a set of real numbers with the property that any number that lies between two numbers in the set is also included in the set. For example, the set of all numbers x satisfying $0 \leq x \leq 1$ is an _____ which contains 0 and 1, as well as all numbers between them. Other examples of _____s are the set of all real numbers $\mathbb{R}$, the set of all positive real numbers, and the empty set.

   a. Ideal
   b. Annihilator
   c. Order
   d. Interval

15. In mathematics, a _____ is, informally, an infinitely vast and infinitely thin sheet. _____s may be thought of as objects in some higher dimensional space, or they may be considered without any outside space, as in the setting of Euclidean geometry

   a. Bandwidth
   b. Blocking
   c. Group
   d. Plane

16. In mathematics a _____ is an inequality which involves a linear function.

When operating in terms of real numbers, linear inequalities are the ones written in the forms

$$f(x) < b \text{ or } f(x) \leq b,$$

where f(x) is a linear functional in real numbers and b is a constant real number. Alternatively, these may be viewed as

$$g(x) < 0 \text{ or } g(x) \leq 0,$$

where g(x) is an affine function.

a. Split-complex number
b. Generalized singular value decomposition
c. Levi-Civita symbol
d. Linear inequality

17. A _____ typically refers to a class of handheld calculators that are capable of plotting graphs, solving simultaneous equations, and performing numerous other tasks with variables. Most popular _____s are also programmable, allowing the user to create customized programs, typically for scientific/engineering and education applications. Due to their large displays intended for graphing, they can also accommodate several lines of text and calculations at a time.
a. Support vector machines
b. Genus
c. Bump mapping
d. Graphing calculator

Chapter 4. LINEAR PROGRAMMING

18. _____ or amortisation is the process of decreasing an amount over a period of time. The word comes from Middle English amortisen to kill, alienate in mortmain, from Anglo-French amorteser, alteration of amortir, from Vulgar Latin admortire to kill, from Latin ad- + mort-, mors death. Particular instances of the term include:

- _____, the allocation of a lump sum amount to different time periods, particularly for loans and other forms of finance, including related interest or other finance charges.
    - _____ schedule, a table detailing each periodic payment on a loan, as generated by an _____ calculator.
    - Negative _____, an _____ schedule where the loan amount actually increases through not paying the full interest
- Amortized analysis, analyzing the execution cost of algorithms over a sequence of operations.
- _____ of capital expenditures of certain assets under accounting rules, particularly intangible assets, in a manner analogous to depreciation.
- _____

_____ is also used in the context of zoning regulations and describes the time in which a property owner has to relocate when the property's use constitutes a preexisting nonconforming use under zoning regulations.

- Depreciation

a. Identity
b. ISAAC
c. Origin
d. Amortization

19. An _____ is a table detailing each periodic payment on a amortizing loan, as generated by an amortization calculator.

While a portion of every payment is applied towards both the interest and the principal balance of the loan, the exact amount applied to principal each time varies. An _____ reveals the specific monetary amount put towards interest, as well as the specific put towards the Principal balance, with each payment.

a. Accounts receivable
b. A Mathematical Theory of Communication
c. A chemical equation
d. Amortization schedule

20. A _____ is a device for performing mathematical calculations, distinguished from a computer by having a limited problem solving ability and an interface optimized for interactive calculation rather than programming. _____s can be hardware or software, and mechanical or electronic, and are often built into devices such as PDAs or mobile phones.

Modern electronic _____s are generally small, digital, and usually inexpensive.

   a. 1-center problem
   b. 120-cell
   c. 2-3 heap
   d. Calculator

21. A set S of real numbers is called _____ from above if there is a real number k such that k ≥ s for all s in S. The number k is called an upper bound of S. The terms _____ from below and lower bound are similarly defined.
   a. Harmonic series
   b. Descent
   c. Derivative algebra
   d. Bounded

22. In optimization, a candidate solution is a member of a set of possible solutions to a given problem. A candidate solution does not have to be a likely or reasonable solution to the problem. The space of all candidate solutions is called the _____, feasible set, search space, or solution space.
   a. Step response
   b. Feasible region
   c. Quadratic eigenvalue problem
   d. Leapfrog integration

23. In mathematics, _____ and undefined are used to explain whether or not expressions have meaningful, sensible, and unambiguous values. Not all branches of mathematics come to the same conclusion.

The following expressions are undefined in all contexts, but remarks in the analysis section may apply.

   a. Plugging in
   b. LHS
   c. Toy model
   d. Defined

24. An _____ is a tree data structure in which each internal node has up to eight children. _____s are most often used to partition a three dimensional space by recursively subdividing it into eight octants. _____s are the three-dimensional analog of quadtrees.

Chapter 4. LINEAR PROGRAMMING

a. Interval tree
b. External node
c. Octree
d. Adaptive k-d tree

25. In mathematics and computer science, an optimization problem is the problem of finding the best solution from all feasible solutions. More formally, an optimization problem A is a quadruple , where

- I is a set of instances;
- given an instance >, f is the set of feasible solutions;
- given an instance x and a feasible solution y of x, m denotes the measure of y, which is usually a positive real.
- g is the goal function, and is either min or max.

The goal is then to find for some instance x an _____, that is, a feasible solution y with

>

For each optimization problem, there is a corresponding decision problem that asks whether there is a feasible solution for some particular measure m_0. For example, if there is a graph G which contains vertices u and v, an optimization problem might be 'find a path from u to v that uses the fewest edges'. This problem might have an answer of, say, 4.

a. Exponential time
b. Optimal solution
c. Approximation algorithms
d. Interactive proof system

26. The mathematical concept of a _____ expresses the intuitive idea of deterministic dependence between two quantities, one of which is viewed as primary and the other as secondary. A _____ then is a way to associate a unique output for each input of a specified type, for example, a real number or an element of a given set.

a. Going up
b. Coherent
c. Grill
d. Function

Chapter 4. LINEAR PROGRAMMING

27. In mathematics, the _____ is an approach to finding a particular solution to certain inhomogeneous ordinary differential equations and recurrence relations. It is closely related to the annihilator method, but instead of using a particular kind of differential operator in order to find the best possible form of the particular solution, a 'guess' is made as to the appropriate form, which is then tested by differentiating the resulting equation. In this sense, the _____ is less formal but more intuitive than the annihilator method.
    a. Phase line
    b. Differential algebraic equations
    c. Linear differential equation
    d. Method of undetermined coefficients

28. In mathematics, a _____ is a statement that can be proved on the basis of explicitly stated or previously agreed assumptions.
    a. Theorem
    b. Boolean function
    c. Disjunction introduction
    d. Logical value

29. In set theory, a _____ is a partially ordered set such that for each t ∈ T, the set {s ∈ T : s < t} is well-ordered by the relation <. For each t ∈ T, the order type of {s ∈ T : s < t} is called the height of t. The height of T itself is the least ordinal greater than the height of each element of T.
    a. Transitive reduction
    b. Definable numbers
    c. Set-theoretic topology
    d. Tree

30. A _____ is a software program that facilitates symbolic mathematics. The core functionality of a CAS is manipulation of mathematical expressions in symbolic form.

Chapter 4. LINEAR PROGRAMMING

The symbolic manipulations supported typically include

- simplification to the smallest possible expression or some standard form, including automatic simplification with assumptions and simplification with constraints
- substitution of symbolic, functors or numeric values for expressions
- change of form of expressions: expanding products and powers, partial and full factorization, rewriting as partial fractions, constraint satisfaction, rewriting trigonometric functions as exponentials, etc.
- partial and total differentiation
- symbolic constrained and unconstrained global optimization
- solution of linear and some non-linear equations over various domains
- solution of some differential and difference equations
- taking some limits
- some indefinite and definite integration, including multidimensional integrals
- integral transforms
- arbitrary-precision numeric operations
- Series operations such as expansion, summation and products
- matrix operations including products, inverses, etc.
- display of mathematical expressions in two-dimensional mathematical form, often using typesetting systems similar to TeX
- add-ons for use in applied mathematics such as physics packages for physical computation
- plotting graphs and parametric plots of functions in two and three dimensions, and animating them
- APIs for linking it on an external program such as a database, or using in a programming language to use the _____
- drawing charts and diagrams
- string manipulation such as matching and searching
- statistical computation
- Theorem proving and verification
- graphic production and editing such as CGI and signal processing as image processing
- sound synthesis

Many also include a programming language, allowing users to implement their own algorithms.

Some _____s focus on a specific area of application; these are typically developed in academia and are free.

a. 2-3 heap
b. 120-cell
c. 1-center problem
d. Computer algebra system

Chapter 4. LINEAR PROGRAMMING

31. A _____ is a 2D geometric symbolic representation of information according to some visualization technique. Sometimes, the technique uses a 3D visualization which is then projected onto the 2D surface. The word graph is sometimes used as a synonym for _____.
   a. 1-center problem
   b. 2-3 heap
   c. Diagram
   d. 120-cell

32. _____ is an economics theory, that refers to individuals or societies gaining the maximum amount out of the resources they have available to them. The theory proposed by most economists is that _____ refers to the _____ of profit.

As some economists have begun to find out, this theory does not hold true for all people and cultures.

   a. Composite
   b. Boundary
   c. Homogeneity
   d. Maximization

33. In Linear programming a _____ is a variable which is added to a constraint to turn the inequality into an equation. This is required to turn an inequality into an equality where a linear combination of variables is less than or equal to a given constant in the former. As with the other variables in the augmented constraints, the _____ cannot take on negative values, as the Simplex algorithm requires them to be positive or zero.
   a. Bellman equation
   b. Shape optimization
   c. Shekel function
   d. Slack variable

34. In the fields of science, engineering, industry and statistics, _____ is the degree of closeness of a measured or calculated quantity to its actual value. _____ is closely related to precision, also called reproducibility or repeatability, the degree to which further measurements or calculations show the same or similar results. The results of calculations or a measurement can be accurate but not precise; precise but not accurate; neither; or both.
   a. A chemical equation
   b. A Mathematical Theory of Communication
   c. A posteriori
   d. Accuracy

Chapter 4. LINEAR PROGRAMMING

35. In mathematics, an _____, or central tendency of a data set refers to a measure of the 'middle' or 'expected' value of the data set. There are many different descriptive statistics that can be chosen as a measurement of the central tendency of the data items.

An _____ is a single value that is meant to typify a list of values.

   a. A posteriori
   b. A Mathematical Theory of Communication
   c. A chemical equation
   d. Average

36. Initial objects are also called _____, and terminal objects are also called final.
   a. Terminal object
   b. Coterminal
   c. Colimit
   d. Direct limit

37. In linear algebra, _____ is a version of Gaussian elimination that puts zeros both above and below each pivot element as it goes from the top row of the given matrix to the bottom. In other words, _____ brings a matrix to reduced row echelon form, whereas Gaussian elimination takes it only as far as row echelon form. Every matrix has a reduced row echelon form, and this algorithm is guaranteed to produce it.
   a. Gauss-Jordan elimination
   b. Spheroidal wave functions
   c. Lax equivalence theorem
   d. Conservation form

38. A _____ is an algebraic equation in which each term is either a constant or the product of a constant and a single variable. _____s can have one, two, three or more variables.

_____s occur with great regularity in applied mathematics.

   a. Linear equation
   b. Quartic equation
   c. Difference of two squares
   d. Quadratic equation

39. The _____ Evaluation and Review Technique, commonly abbreviated PERT, is a model for project management designed to analyze and represent the tasks involved in completing a given project.

Chapter 4. LINEAR PROGRAMMING

PERT is a method to analyze the involved tasks in completing a given project, especially the time needed to complete each task, and identifying the minimum time needed to complete the total project.

This model was invented by Booz Allen Hamilton, Inc.

a. Huge
b. Key server
c. Battle of the Sexes
d. Program

40. In Linear programming a _____ is a variable which is subtracted from a constraint to turn the inequality into an equation.

This is required to turn an inequality into an equality where a linear combination of variables is greater than or equal to a given constant in the former. As with the other variables in the augmented constraints, the _____ cannot take on negative values, as the Simplex algorithm requires them to be positive or zero.

a. Quantum annealing
b. Successive linear programming
c. Global optimum
d. Surplus variable

41. In the geometry of the projective plane, _____ refers to geometric transformations that replace points by lines and lines by points while preserving incidence properties among the transformed objects. The existence of such transformations leads to a general principle, that any theorem about incidences between points and lines in the projective plane may be transformed into another theorem about lines and points, by a substitution of the appropriate words.

_____ in the projective plane is a special case of _____ for projective spaces, transformations that interchange

dimension + codimension.

a. Duality
b. Disk
c. Decidable
d. Blocking

Chapter 4. LINEAR PROGRAMMING

42. In the mathematical area of order theory, every partially ordered set P gives rise to a _____ partially ordered set which is often denoted by P^op or P^d. This _____ order P^op is defined to be the set with the inverse order. It is easy to see that this construction, which can be depicted by flipping the Hasse diagram for P upside down, will indeed yield a partially ordered set.
   a. Christofides heuristics
   b. Contraction mapping
   c. Context-sensitive language
   d. Dual

43. In linear programming, the primary problem and the _____ are complementary. A solution to either one determines a solution to both.

    Linear programming problems are optimization problems in which the objective function and the constraints are all linear.

   a. Linear programming relaxation
   b. Dual problem
   c. Linear matrix inequality
   d. Topological derivative

44. A _____ is an abstract model that uses mathematical language to describe the behavior of a system. Eykhoff defined a _____ as 'a representation of the essential aspects of an existing system which presents knowledge of that system in usable form'.
   a. Total least squares
   b. Rata Die
   c. Metaheuristic
   d. Mathematical model

45. In informal language, a _____ is a function that swaps two elements of a set. More formally, given a finite set $X = \{a_1, a_2, \ldots, a_n\}$, a _____ is a permutation f, such that there exist indices i,j such that fj, fi and fk for all other indices k. This is often denoted as

For example, if X = {a,b,c,d,e}, the function σ given by

$$\sigma(a) = a$$
$$\sigma(b) = e$$
$$\sigma(c) = c$$
$$\sigma(d) = d$$
$$\sigma(e) = b$$

is a _____.

Any permutation can be expressed as the composition of _____s.

a. Chiral
b. Bounded
c. C-35
d. Transposition

46. In economics, business, retail, and accounting, a _____ is the value of money that has been used up to produce something, and hence is not available for use anymore. In business, the _____ may be one of acquisition, in which case the amount of money expended to acquire it is counted as _____. In this case, money is the input that is gone in order to acquire the thing.
a. 120-cell
b. 2-3 heap
c. 1-center problem
d. Cost

Chapter 5. THE MATHEMATICS OF FINANCE

1. _____ is a fee, paid on borrowed capital. Assets lent include money, shares, consumer goods through hire purchase, major assets such as aircraft, and even entire factories in finance lease arrangements. The _____ is calculated upon the value of the assets in the same manner as upon money.

   a. A Mathematical Theory of Communication
   b. Interest expense
   c. Interest
   d. Interest sensitivity gap

2. The _____ of a number are those digits that carry meaning contributing to its precision. This includes all digits except:

   - leading and trailing zeros where they serve merely as placeholders to indicate the scale of the number.
   - spurious digits introduced, for example, by calculations carried out to greater accuracy than that of the original data, or measurements reported to a greater precision than the equipment supports.

   The concept of _____ is often used in connection with rounding. Rounding to n _____ is a more general-purpose technique than rounding to n decimal places, since it handles numbers of different scales in a uniform way. A practical calculation that uses any irrational number necessitates rounding the number, and hence the answer, to a finite number of _____.

   a. Tetration
   b. Rounding
   c. Significant figures
   d. Shabakh

3. In mathematics, _____ and undefined are used to explain whether or not expressions have meaningful, sensible, and unambiguous values. Not all branches of mathematics come to the same conclusion.

   The following expressions are undefined in all contexts, but remarks in the analysis section may apply.

   a. Plugging in
   b. Toy model
   c. LHS
   d. Defined

4. In mathematics, the _____ is a term used to describe the number of times one must apply a given operation to an integer before reaching a fixed point.

   Usually, this refers to the additive or multiplicative persistence of an integer, which is how often one has to replace the number by the sum or product of its digits until one reaches a single digit. Because the numbers are broken down into their digits, the additive or multiplicative persistence depends on the radix.

Chapter 5. THE MATHEMATICS OF FINANCE

    a. Lychrel number
    b. Persistence of a number
    c. Linear congruence theorem
    d. Coprime

5. In abstract algebra, a module S over a ring R is called _____ or irreducible if it is not the zero module 0 and if its only submodules are 0 and S. Understanding the _____ modules over a ring is usually helpful because these modules form the 'building blocks' of all other modules in a certain sense.

Abelian groups are the same as Z-modules.

    a. Basis
    b. Derivation
    c. Harmonic series
    d. Simple

6. A _____ is a mathematical model of a system based on the use of a linear operator. _____s typically exhibit features and properties that are much simpler than the general, nonlinear case. As a mathematical abstraction or idealization, _____s find important applications in automatic control theory, signal processing, and telecommunications.

    a. Hybrid system
    b. Percolation
    c. Predispositioning Theory
    d. Linear system

7. _____ involves reducing the number of significant digits in a number. The result of _____ is a 'shorter' number having fewer non-zero digits yet similar in magnitude. The result is less precise but easier to use.

    a. Hyper operator
    b. Sudan function
    c. Shabakh
    d. Rounding

8. In linear algebra, a _____ is a set of vectors that, in a linear combination, can represent every vector in a given vector space or free module, and such that no element of the set can be represented as a linear combination of the others. In other words, a _____ is a linearly independent spanning set. This picture illustrates the standard _____ in R^2.

a. Conchoid
b. Chiral
c. Dot plot
d. Basis

9. _____ is the concept of adding accumulated interest back to the principal, so that interest is earned on interest from that moment on. The act of declaring interest to be principal is called compounding. A loan, for example, may have its interest compounded every month: in this case, a loan with $100 principal and 1% interest per month would have a balance of $101 at the end of the first month.
a. Compound interest
b. Net interest margin securities
c. Net interest margin
d. Retained interest

10. The _____ is a function in mathematics. The application of this function to a value x is written as ex. Equivalently, this can be written in the form e^x, where e is a mathematical constant, the base of the natural logarithm, which equals approximately 2.718281828, and is also known as Euler's number.
a. Exponential function
b. A chemical equation
c. Area hyperbolic functions
d. A Mathematical Theory of Communication

11. The mathematical concept of a _____ expresses the intuitive idea of deterministic dependence between two quantities, one of which is viewed as primary and the other as secondary. A _____ then is a way to associate a unique output for each input of a specified type, for example, a real number or an element of a given set.
a. Function
b. Grill
c. Going up
d. Coherent

12. In mathematics, a _____ is a number that can be expressed as an integral of an algebraic function over an algebraic domain. Kontsevich and Zagier define a _____ as a complex number whose real and imaginary parts are values of absolutely convergent integrals of rational functions with rational coefficients, over domains in given by polynomial inequalities with rational coefficients.

Chapter 5. THE MATHEMATICS OF FINANCE

a. Boussinesq approximation
b. Closeness
c. Period
d. Disk

13. A _____ typically refers to a class of handheld calculators that are capable of plotting graphs, solving simultaneous equations, and performing numerous other tasks with variables. Most popular _____s are also programmable, allowing the user to create customized programs, typically for scientific/engineering and education applications. Due to their large displays intended for graphing, they can also accommodate several lines of text and calculations at a time.

a. Bump mapping
b. Genus
c. Support vector machines
d. Graphing calculator

14. _____ or amortisation is the process of decreasing an amount over a period of time. The word comes from Middle English amortisen to kill, alienate in mortmain, from Anglo-French amorteser, alteration of amortir, from Vulgar Latin admortire to kill, from Latin ad- + mort-, mors death. Particular instances of the term include:

- _____, the allocation of a lump sum amount to different time periods, particularly for loans and other forms of finance, including related interest or other finance charges.
    - _____ schedule, a table detailing each periodic payment on a loan, as generated by an _____ calculator.
    - Negative _____, an _____ schedule where the loan amount actually increases through not paying the full interest
- Amortized analysis, analyzing the execution cost of algorithms over a sequence of operations.
- _____ of capital expenditures of certain assets under accounting rules, particularly intangible assets, in a manner analogous to depreciation.
- _____

_____ is also used in the context of zoning regulations and describes the time in which a property owner has to relocate when the property's use constitutes a preexisting nonconforming use under zoning regulations.

- Depreciation

a. ISAAC
b. Identity
c. Amortization
d. Origin

Chapter 5. THE MATHEMATICS OF FINANCE

15. An _____ is a table detailing each periodic payment on a amortizing loan, as generated by an amortization calculator.

While a portion of every payment is applied towards both the interest and the principal balance of the loan, the exact amount applied to principal each time varies. An _____ reveals the specific monetary amount put towards interest, as well as the specific put towards the Principal balance, with each payment.

a. A Mathematical Theory of Communication
b. Accounts receivable
c. A chemical equation
d. Amortization schedule

16. A _____ is a device for performing mathematical calculations, distinguished from a computer by having a limited problem solving ability and an interface optimized for interactive calculation rather than programming. _____s can be hardware or software, and mechanical or electronic, and are often built into devices such as PDAs or mobile phones.

Modern electronic _____s are generally small, digital, and usually inexpensive.

a. 2-3 heap
b. 120-cell
c. Calculator
d. 1-center problem

17. In mathematics, the _____ is a direct product of sets. The _____ is named after René Descartes, whose formulation of analytic geometry gave rise to this concept.

Specifically, the _____ of two sets X and Y, denoted X × Y, is the set of all possible ordered pairs whose first component is a member of X and whose second component is a member of Y:

$$X \times Y = \{(x,y) | x \in X \text{ and } y \in Y\}.$$

For example, the _____ of the 13-element set of standard playing card ranks {Ace, King, Queen, Jack, 10, 9, 8, 7, 6, 5, 4, 3, 2} and the four-element set of card suits {â™ , â™¥, â™¦, â™£} is the 52-element set of all possible playing cards ,, ...,, ...,}.

a. Set of all sets
b. Disjoint sets
c. Choice function
d. Cartesian product

Chapter 5. THE MATHEMATICS OF FINANCE

18. The _____ Evaluation and Review Technique, commonly abbreviated PERT, is a model for project management designed to analyze and represent the tasks involved in completing a given project.

PERT is a method to analyze the involved tasks in completing a given project, especially the time needed to complete each task, and identifying the minimum time needed to complete the total project.

This model was invented by Booz Allen Hamilton, Inc.

   a. Huge
   b. Key server
   c. Battle of the Sexes
   d. Program

19. _____ expresses an annual rate of interest taking into account the effect of compounding, usually for deposit or investment products. It is analogous to the Annual percentage rate, which is used for loans. In some jurisdictions, the use and definition of _____ may be regulated by a government agency, in which case it would generally be capitalized.
   a. A Mathematical Theory of Communication
   b. Annual percentage yield
   c. A chemical equation
   d. A posteriori

20. In mathematics, a _____ is a way of expressing a number as a fraction of 100. It is often denoted using the percent sign, '%'. For example, 45% is equal to 45 / 100, or 0.45.
   a. Lowest common denominator
   b. Subtrahend
   c. Least common multiple
   d. Percentage

21. In computational complexity theory, an algorithm is said to take _____ if the asymptotic upper bound for the time it requires is proportional to the size of the input, which is usually denoted n.

Informally spoken, the running time increases linearly with the size of the input. For example, a procedure that adds up all elements of a list requires time proportional to the length of the list.

   a. Linear time
   b. Truth table reduction
   c. Constructible function
   d. Time-constructible function

Chapter 5. THE MATHEMATICS OF FINANCE

22. _____ is a term used in accounting, economics and finance to spread the cost of an asset over the span of several years.

In simple words we can say that _____ is the reduction in the value of an asset due to usage, passage of time, wear and tear, technological outdating or obsolescence, depletion or other such factors.

In accounting, _____ is a term used to describe any method of attributing the historical or purchase cost of an asset across its useful life, roughly corresponding to normal wear and tear.

   a. 1-center problem
   b. 120-cell
   c. Gross sales
   d. Depreciation

23. In calculus, a function f defined on a subset of the real numbers with real values is called monotonic (also monotonically increasing or non-_____), if for all x and y such that x ≤ y one has f(x) ≤ f(y), so f preserves the order. In layman's terms, the sign of the slope is always positive (the curve tending upwards) or zero (i.e., non-_____, or asymptotic, or depicted as a horizontal, flat line) Likewise, a function is called monotonically _____ (non-increasing) if, whenever x ≤ y, then f(x) ≥ f(y), so it reverses the order.
   a. Tensor product of Hilbert spaces
   b. Circular convolution
   c. Dual pair
   d. Decreasing

24. In mathematics, a _____ is a series with a constant ratio between successive terms. For example, the series

$$\frac{1}{2} + \frac{1}{4} + \frac{1}{8} + \frac{1}{16} + \cdots$$

is geometric, because each term is equal to half of the previous term. The sum of this series is 1, as illustrated in the following picture:

_____ are one of the simplest examples of infinite series with finite sums.

   a. Telescoping series
   b. Riemann series theorem
   c. Summation by parts
   d. Geometric series

Chapter 5. THE MATHEMATICS OF FINANCE

25. In mathematics, a _____ is often represented as the sum of a sequence of terms. That is, a _____ is represented as a list of numbers with addition operations between them, for example this arithmetic sequence:

   1 + 2 + 3 + 4 + 5 + ... + 99 + 100

In most cases of interest the terms of the sequence are produced according to a certain rule, such as by a formula, by an algorithm, by a sequence of measurements, or even by a random number generator.

   a. Series
   b. Concavity
   c. Contact
   d. Blind

26. In scientific inquiry, an _____ is a method of investigating particular types of research questions or solving particular types of problems. The _____ is a cornerstone in the empirical approach to acquiring deeper knowledge about the world and is used in both natural sciences as well as in social sciences. An _____ is defined, in science, as a method of investigating less known fields, solving practical problems and proving theoretical assumptions.

   a. A chemical equation
   b. A Mathematical Theory of Communication
   c. A posteriori
   d. Experiment

27. A _____ is the transfer of an interest in property (or in law the equivalent - a charge) to a lender as a security for a debt - usually a loan of money. While a _____ in itself is not a debt, it is lender's security for a debt. It is a transfer of an interest in land (or the equivalent), from the owner to the _____ lender, on the condition that this interest will be returned to the owner of the real estate when the terms of the _____ have been satisfied or performed.

   a. Mortgage
   b. 1-center problem
   c. 2-3 heap
   d. 120-cell

28. In finance, _____ rate of profit or sometimes just return, is the ratio of money gained or lost on an investment relative to the amount of money invested. The amount of money gained or lost may be referred to as interest, profit/loss, gain/loss, or net income/loss. The money invested may be referred to as the asset, capital, principal, or the cost basis of the investment.

a. Return on equity
b. 1-center problem
c. P/E ratio
d. Rate of return

Chapter 6. SETS AND COUNTING

1. A _____ undone, which forms a cube _____ cube; a type of _____

A _____ is a problem or enigma that challenges ingenuity. In a basic _____ one is intended to piece together objects (_____ pieces) in a logical way in order to come up with the desired shape, picture or solution. _____s are often contrived as a form of entertainment, but they can also stem from serious mathematical or logistical problems -- in such cases, their successful resolution can be a significant contribution to mathematical research.

   a. The Doctrine of Chances
   b. Visible
   c. The Code Book
   d. Puzzle

2. _____ is a branch of pure mathematics concerning the study of discrete objects. It is related to many other areas of mathematics, such as algebra, probability theory, ergodic theory and geometry, as well as to applied subjects in computer science and statistical physics. Aspects of _____ include 'counting' the objects satisfying certain criteria, deciding when the criteria can be met, and constructing and analyzing objects meeting the criteria, finding 'largest', 'smallest', or 'optimal' objects, and finding algebraic structures these objects may have.
   a. Combinatorics
   b. Restricted sumset
   c. Factorial
   d. Combinatorial species

3. In mathematics, an _____ or member of a set is any one of the distinct objects that make up that set.

Writing A = {1,2,3,4}, means that the _____s of the set A are the numbers 1, 2, 3 and 4. Groups of _____s of A, for example {1,2}, are subsets of A.

   a. Ideal
   b. Order
   c. Universal code
   d. Element

4. In mathematics, especially in set theory, a set A is a _____ of a set B if A is 'contained' inside B. Notice that A and B may coincide. The relationship of one set being a _____ of another is called inclusion.
   a. Set of all sets
   b. Horizontal line test
   c. Subset
   d. Cartesian product

Chapter 6. SETS AND COUNTING

5. _____ are small polyhedral objects, usually cubic, used for generating random numbers or other symbols. This makes _____ suitable as gambling devices, especially for craps or sic bo, or for use in non-gambling tabletop games.

A traditional die is a cube, marked on each of its six faces with a different number of circular patches or pits called pips.

   a. 2-3 heap
   b. 1-center problem
   c. 120-cell
   d. Dice

6. In mathematics, and more specifically set theory, the _____ is the unique set having no members. Some axiomatic set theories assure that the _____ exists by including an axiom of _____; in other theories, its existence can be deduced. Many possible properties of sets are trivially true for the _____.
   a. A Mathematical Theory of Communication
   b. Inverse function
   c. Empty function
   d. Empty set

7. _____ or set diagrams are diagrams that show all hypothetically possible logical relations between a finite collection of sets. _____ were invented around 1880 by John Venn. They are used in many fields, including set theory, probability, logic, statistics, and computer science.
   a. 120-cell
   b. 1-center problem
   c. 2-3 heap
   d. Venn diagrams

8. A _____ is a 2D geometric symbolic representation of information according to some visualization technique. Sometimes, the technique uses a 3D visualization which is then projected onto the 2D surface. The word graph is sometimes used as a synonym for _____.
   a. 2-3 heap
   b. 120-cell
   c. 1-center problem
   d. Diagram

9. The _____ are the set of numbers consisting of the natural numbers including 0 and their negatives. They are numbers that can be written without a fractional or decimal component, and fall within the set {... −2, −1, 0, 1, 2, ...}.

a. A chemical equation
b. A posteriori
c. A Mathematical Theory of Communication
d. Integers

10. In discrete mathematics and predominantly in set theory, a _____ is a concept used in comparisons of sets to refer to the unique values of one set in relation to another. The terms 'absolute' and 'relative' _____ refer to more specific applications of the concept, with universal _____s referring to elements unique to the universal set and the latter referring to the unique elements of one set in relation to another. In this image, the universal set is represented by the border of the image, and the set A as a disc.
   a. Derivative algebra
   b. Kernel
   c. Huge
   d. Complement

11. In mathematics, the _____ of two sets A and B is the set that contains all elements of A that also belong to B, but no other elements.

For explanation of the symbols used in this article, refer to the table of mathematical symbols.

The _____ of A and B

The _____ of A and B is written 'A ∩ B'. Formally:

>   x is an element of A ∩ B if and only if
>   - x is an element of A and
>   - x is an element of B.
>
>   For example:
>   - The _____ of the sets {1, 2, 3} and {2, 3, 4} is {2, 3}.
>   - The number 9 is not in the _____ of the set of prime numbers {2, 3, 5, 7, 11, â€¦} and the set of odd numbers {1, 3, 5, 7, 9, 11, â€¦}.

If the _____ of two sets A and B is empty, that is they have no elements in common, then they are said to be disjoint, denoted: A ∩ B = Ø. For example the sets {1, 2} and {3, 4} are disjoint, written {1, 2} ∩ {3, 4} = Ø.

a. Advice
b. Erlang
c. Order
d. Intersection

12. In set theory, the term _____ refers to a set operation used in the convergence of set elements to form a resultant set containing the elements of both sets. As a simple example, a _____ of two disjoint sets, which do not have elements in common results in a set containing all elements from both sets. A Venn diagram representing the _____ of sets A and B.
   a. Union
   b. Event
   c. Introduction
   d. UES

13. In mathematics, _____ is a technique for optimization of a linear objective function, subject to linear equality and linear inequality constraints. Informally, _____ determines the way to achieve the best outcome in a given mathematical model given some list of requirements represented as linear equations.

More formally, given a polytope, and a real-valued affine function

$$f(x_1, x_2, \ldots, x_n) = c_1 x_1 + c_2 x_2 + \cdots + c_n x_n + d$$

defined on this polytope, a _____ method will find a point in the polytope where this function has the smallest value.

   a. Linear programming
   b. Lin-Kernighan
   c. Descent direction
   d. Linear programming relaxation

14. _____ is a complete system for logical operations. It was named after George Boole, who first defined an algebraic system of logic in the mid 19th century. _____ has many applications in electronics, computer hardware and software, and is the base of digital electronics.
   a. Reed-Muller expansion
   b. Boolean datatype
   c. Zhegalkin polynomials
   d. Boolean logic

15. In mathematics, the _____ is a direct product of sets. The _____ is named after René Descartes, whose formulation of analytic geometry gave rise to this concept.

Specifically, the _____ of two sets X and Y, denoted X × Y, is the set of all possible ordered pairs whose first component is a member of X and whose second component is a member of Y:

$$X \times Y = \{(x,y) | x \in X \text{ and } y \in Y\}.$$

For example, the _____ of the 13-element set of standard playing card ranks {Ace, King, Queen, Jack, 10, 9, 8, 7, 6, 5, 4, 3, 2} and the four-element set of card suits {♠, ♥, ♦, ♣} is the 52-element set of all possible playing cards ,, ...,,, ...,,}.

 a. Cartesian product
 b. Disjoint sets
 c. Set of all sets
 d. Choice function

16. In mathematics, two sets are said to be disjoint if they have no element in common. For example, {1, 2, 3} and {4, 5, 6} are _____.

Formally, two sets A and B are disjoint if their intersection is the empty set. wikimedia.org/math/b/3/5/b35d3befc06b831ff4d6cd63bf922efb.png">

This definition extends to any collection of sets.

 a. Horizontal line test
 b. Preimage
 c. Subset
 d. Disjoint sets

17. In quantum field theory and statistical mechanics in the thermodynamic limit, a system with a global symmetry can have more than one phase. For parameters where the symmetry is spontaneously broken, the system is said to be _____. When the global symmetry is unbroken the system is disordered.
 a. Einstein relation
 b. Ordered
 c. Ursell function
 d. Isoenthalpic-isobaric ensemble

18. In mathematics, an _____ is a collection of objects having two coordinates (or entries or projections), such that one can always uniquely determine the object, which is the first coordinate (or first entry or left projection) of the pair as well as the second coordinate (or second entry or right projection.) If the first coordinate is a and the second is b, the usual notation for an _____ is (a, b.) The pair is 'ordered' in that (a, b) differs from (b, a) unless a = b.

a. A posteriori
b. A chemical equation
c. A Mathematical Theory of Communication
d. Ordered pair

19. A _____ is a device for performing mathematical calculations, distinguished from a computer by having a limited problem solving ability and an interface optimized for interactive calculation rather than programming. _____s can be hardware or software, and mechanical or electronic, and are often built into devices such as PDAs or mobile phones.

Modern electronic _____s are generally small, digital, and usually inexpensive.

a. 2-3 heap
b. Calculator
c. 1-center problem
d. 120-cell

20. In set theory, a _____ (or discriminated union) is a modified union operation which indexes the elements according to which set they originated in.

Formally, let $\{A_i : i \in I\}$ be a family of sets indexed by I. The _____ of this family is the set

$$\coprod_{i \in I} A_i = \bigcup_{i \in I} \{(x, i) : x \in A_i\}.$$

The elements of the _____ are ordered pairs (x, i.)

a. Cartesian product
b. Preimage
c. Disjoint union
d. Disjoint sets

21. In mathematics, the _____ of a set is a measure of the 'number of elements of the set'. For example, the set A = {1, 2, 3} contains 3 elements, and therefore A has a _____ of 3. There are two approaches to _____ - one which compares sets directly using bijections and injections, and another which uses cardinal numbers.

a. 1-center problem
b. 2-3 heap
c. Cardinality
d. 120-cell

22. In game theory, an _____ is a set of moves or strategies taken by the players, or their payoffs resulting from the actions or strategies taken by all players. The two are complementary in that given knowledge of the set of strategies of all players, the final state of the game is known, as are any relevant payoffs. In a game where chance or a random event is involved, the _____ is not known from only the set of strategies, but is only realized when the random even are realized.
   a. Outcome
   b. Algebraic
   c. Equaliser
   d. Autonomous system

23. _____ is the mathematical operation of scaling one number by another. It is one of the four basic operations in elementary arithmetic.

_____ is defined for whole numbers in terms of repeated addition; for example, 4 multiplied by 3 can be calculated by adding 3 copies of 4 together:

$$4 + 4 + 4 = 12.$$

_____ of rational numbers and real numbers is defined by systematic generalization of this basic idea.

   a. The number 0 is even.
   b. Least common multiple
   c. Highest common factor
   d. Multiplication

24. In mathematics, computing, linguistics and related subjects, an _____ is a sequence of finite instructions, often used for calculation and data processing. It is formally a type of effective method in which a list of well-defined instructions for completing a task will, when given an initial state, proceed through a well-defined series of successive states, eventually terminating in an end-state. The transition from one state to the next is not necessarily deterministic; some _____s, known as probabilistic _____s, incorporate randomness.
   a. Approximate counting algorithm
   b. In-place algorithm
   c. Out-of-core
   d. Algorithm

Chapter 6. SETS AND COUNTING

25. _____ occurs when the identities of two or more individuals, concepts sharing some characteristics of one another, become confused until there seems to be only a single identity.

In language, idiom _____ is the amalgamation of two different expressions. In most cases, the combination results in a new expression that makes little sense literally, but clearly expresses an idea because it references well-known idioms.

- a. Finitism
- b. Conflation
- c. Validity
- d. Proof theory

26. In operations research, specifically in decision analysis, a _____ is a decision support tool that uses a graph or model of decisions and their possible consequences, including chance event outcomes, resource costs, and utility. A _____ is used to identify the strategy most likely to reach a goal. Another use of trees is as a descriptive means for calculating conditional probabilities.

- a. 1-center problem
- b. Decision tree
- c. 2-3 heap
- d. 120-cell

27. In set theory, a _____ is a partially ordered set such that for each t ∈ T, the set {s ∈ T : s < t} is well-ordered by the relation <. For each t ∈ T, the order type of {s ∈ T : s < t} is called the height of t. The height of T itself is the least ordinal greater than the height of each element of T.

- a. Definable numbers
- b. Set-theoretic topology
- c. Transitive reduction
- d. Tree

28. In several fields of mathematics the term _____ is used with different but closely related meanings. They all relate to the notion of mapping the elements of a set to other elements of the same set, i.e., exchanging elements of a set.

The general concept of _____ can be defined more formally in different contexts:

In combinatorics, a _____ is usually understood to be a sequence containing each element from a finite set once, and only once.

a. Permutation
b. Cyclic permutation
c. Linearly independent
d. Tensor product

29. In mathematics, the _____ of a non-negative integer n, denoted by n!, is the product of all positive integers less than or equal to n. For example,

$$5! = 1 \times 2 \times 3 \times 4 \times 5 = 120$$

and
$$6! = 1 \times 2 \times 3 \times 4 \times 5 \times 6 = 720$$

The notation n! was introduced by Christian Kramp in 1808.

The _____ function is formally defined by

$$n! = \prod_{k=1}^{n} k \quad \forall n \in \mathbb{N}.$$

The above definition incorporates the instance

$$0! = 1$$

as an instance of the fact that the product of no numbers at all is 1.

a. Symbolic combinatorics
b. Plane partition
c. Partition of a set
d. Factorial

30. A _____ typically refers to a class of handheld calculators that are capable of plotting graphs, solving simultaneous equations, and performing numerous other tasks with variables. Most popular _____s are also programmable, allowing the user to create customized programs, typically for scientific/engineering and education applications. Due to their large displays intended for graphing, they can also accommodate several lines of text and calculations at a time.

Chapter 6. SETS AND COUNTING

a. Bump mapping
b. Graphing calculator
c. Genus
d. Support vector machines

31. _____ or amortisation is the process of decreasing an amount over a period of time. The word comes from Middle English amortisen to kill, alienate in mortmain, from Anglo-French amorteser, alteration of amortir, from Vulgar Latin admortire to kill, from Latin ad- + mort-, mors death. Particular instances of the term include:

- _____, the allocation of a lump sum amount to different time periods, particularly for loans and other forms of finance, including related interest or other finance charges.
    - _____ schedule, a table detailing each periodic payment on a loan, as generated by an _____ calculator.
    - Negative _____, an _____ schedule where the loan amount actually increases through not paying the full interest
- Amortized analysis, analyzing the execution cost of algorithms over a sequence of operations.
- _____ of capital expenditures of certain assets under accounting rules, particularly intangible assets, in a manner analogous to depreciation.
- _____

_____ is also used in the context of zoning regulations and describes the time in which a property owner has to relocate when the property's use constitutes a preexisting nonconforming use under zoning regulations.

- Depreciation

a. Origin
b. Amortization
c. ISAAC
d. Identity

32. An _____ is a table detailing each periodic payment on a amortizing loan, as generated by an amortization calculator.

While a portion of every payment is applied towards both the interest and the principal balance of the loan, the exact amount applied to principal each time varies. An _____ reveals the specific monetary amount put towards interest, as well as the specific put towards the Principal balance, with each payment.

86   Chapter 6. SETS AND COUNTING

a. Accounts receivable
b. Amortization schedule
c. A chemical equation
d. A Mathematical Theory of Communication

33. The mathematical concept of a _____ expresses the intuitive idea of deterministic dependence between two quantities, one of which is viewed as primary and the other as secondary. A _____ then is a way to associate a unique output for each input of a specified type, for example, a real number or an element of a given set.

a. Grill
b. Coherent
c. Going up
d. Function

34. In combinatorial mathematics, a _____ is an un-ordered collection of distinct elements, usually of a prescribed size and taken from a given set. Given such a set S, a _____ of elements of S is just a subset of S, where as always forsets the order of the elements is not taken into account. Also, as always forsets, no elements can be repeated more than once in a _____; this is often referred to as a 'collection without repetition'.

a. Combination
b. Fill-in
c. Heawood number
d. Sparsity

35. In elementary algebra, a _____ is a polynomial with two terms: the sum of two monomials. It is the simplest kind of polynomial except for a monomial.

The _____ $a^2 - b^2$ can be factored as the product of two other _____ s:

$a^2 - b^2$.

The product of a pair of linear _____ s a x + b and c x + d is:

2 +x + bd.

A _____ raised to the nth power, represented as

n

can be expanded by means of the _____ theorem or, equivalently, using Pascal's triangle.

a. Cylindrical algebraic decomposition
b. Real structure
c. Rational root theorem
d. Binomial

36. In mathematics, the _____ $\binom{n}{k}$ is the coefficient of the x^k term in the polynomial expansion of the binomial power n.

In combinatorics, $\binom{n}{k}$ is interpreted as the number of k-element subsets of an n-element set, that is the number of ways that k things can be 'chosen' from a set of n things. Hence, $\binom{n}{k}$ is often read as 'n choose k' and called the choose function of n and k.

a. Dyson conjecture
b. Symbolic combinatorics
c. Rule of product
d. Binomial coefficient

37. In mathematics, a _____ is a constant multiplicative factor of a certain object. For example, in the expression $9x^2$, the _____ of x^2 is 9.

The object can be such things as a variable, a vector, a function, etc.

a. Coefficient
b. Multivariate division algorithm
c. Fibonacci polynomials
d. Stability radius

38. In mathematics, the _____ is an important formula giving the expansion of powers of sums. Its simplest version states that

$$(x+y)^n = \sum_{k=0}^{n} \binom{n}{k} x^{n-k} y^k \qquad (1)$$

for any real or complex numbers x and y, and any nonnegative integer n. The binomial coefficient appearing in may be defined in terms of the factorial function n!:

$$\binom{n}{k} = \frac{n!}{k!\,(n-k)!}.$$

For example, here are the cases where 2 ≤ n ≤ 5:

$$(x+y)^2 = x^2 + 2xy + y^2$$
$$(x+y)^3 = x^3 + 3x^2y + 3xy^2 + y^3$$
$$(x+y)^4 = x^4 + 4x^3y + 6x^2y^2 + 4xy^3 + y^4$$
$$(x+y)^5 = x^5 + 5x^4y + 10x^3y^2 + 10x^2y^3 + 5xy^4 + y^5.$$

Formula is valid more generally for any elements x and y of a semiring as long as xy = yx..

a. Lah numbers
b. Stirling transform
c. Hypergeometric identities
d. Binomial theorem

39. In mathematics, a _____ is a statement that can be proved on the basis of explicitly stated or previously agreed assumptions.

a. Logical value
b. Disjunction introduction
c. Boolean function
d. Theorem

Chapter 7. PROBABILITY

1. The _____ is a probability puzzle based on the American television game show Let's Make a Deal. The name comes from the show's host, Monty Hall. The problem is also called the Monty Hall paradox, as it is a veridical paradox in that the solution is counterintuitive.
    a. Zero-point energy
    b. Triquetra
    c. Rock-paper-scissors
    d. Monty Hall problem

2. Introduction

In the theory of probability and statistics, a _____ is an experiment whose outcome is random and can be either of two possible outcomes, 'success' and 'failure'.

In practice it refers to a single experiment which can have one of two possible outcomes. These events can be phrased into 'yes or no' questions:

- Did the coin land heads?
- Was the newborn child a girl?
- Were a person's eyes green?
- Did a mosquito die after the area was sprayed with insecticide?
- Did a potential customer decide to buy a product?
- Did a citizen vote for a specific candidate?
- Did an employee vote pro-union?

Therefore success and failure are labels for outcomes, and should not be construed literally. Examples of _____s include

- Flipping a coin. In this context, obverse conventionally denotes success and reverse denotes failure. A fair coin has the probability of success 0.5 by definition.
- Rolling a die, where a six is 'success' and everything else a 'failure'.
- In conducting a political opinion poll, choosing a voter at random to ascertain whether that voter will vote 'yes' in an upcoming referendum.

Mathematically, a _____ can be described by a sample space Ω consisting of two values, s for 'success' and f for 'failure'. Therefore the sample space is $\Omega = \{s, f\}$.

   a. Point process
   b. Marginal distribution
   c. Law of total cumulance
   d. Bernoulli trial

3. In scientific inquiry, an _____ is a method of investigating particular types of research questions or solving particular types of problems. The _____ is a cornerstone in the empirical approach to acquiring deeper knowledge about the world and is used in both natural sciences as well as in social sciences. An _____ is defined, in science, as a method of investigating less known fields, solving practical problems and proving theoretical assumptions.

   a. A posteriori
   b. Experiment
   c. A Mathematical Theory of Communication
   d. A chemical equation

4. In game theory, an _____ is a set of moves or strategies taken by the players, or their payoffs resulting from the actions or strategies taken by all players. The two are complementary in that given knowledge of the set of strategies of all players, the final state of the game is known, as are any relevant payoffs. In a game where chance or a random event is involved, the _____ is not known from only the set of strategies, but is only realized when the random even are realized.

   a. Outcome
   b. Equaliser
   c. Autonomous system
   d. Algebraic

5. In statistics, a _____ is a subset of a population. Typically, the population is very large, making a census or a complete enumeration of all the values in the population impractical or impossible. The _____ represents a subset of manageable size.

   a. Boussinesq approximation
   b. Duality
   c. Sample
   d. Dispersion

6. In probability theory, the _____ or universal _____, often denoted S, Ω of an experiment or random trial is the set of all possible outcomes. For example, if the experiment is tossing a coin, the _____ is the set {head, tail}. For tossing a single six-sided die, the _____ is {1, 2, 3, 4, 5, 6}.

   a. Marginal distribution
   b. Markov chain
   c. Martingale central limit theorem
   d. Sample space

7. In mathematics, _____ and undefined are used to explain whether or not expressions have meaningful, sensible, and unambiguous values. Not all branches of mathematics come to the same conclusion.

The following expressions are undefined in all contexts, but remarks in the analysis section may apply.

a. Toy model
b. Defined
c. LHS
d. Plugging in

8. In probability theory, an _____ is a set of outcomes to which a probability is assigned. Typically, when the sample space is finite, any subset of the sample space is an _____. However, this approach does not work well in cases where the sample space is infinite, most notably when the outcome is a real number.
   a. Information set
   b. Equaliser
   c. Event
   d. Audio compression

9. In discrete mathematics and predominantly in set theory, a _____ is a concept used in comparisons of sets to refer to the unique values of one set in relation to another. The terms 'absolute' and 'relative' _____ refer to more specific applications of the concept, with universal _____s referring to elements unique to the universal set and the latter referring to the unique elements of one set in relation to another. In this image, the universal set is represented by the border of the image, and the set A as a disc.
   a. Huge
   b. Kernel
   c. Complement
   d. Derivative algebra

10. In mathematics, the _____ of two sets A and B is the set that contains all elements of A that also belong to B, but no other elements.

For explanation of the symbols used in this article, refer to the table of mathematical symbols.

The _____ of A and B

The _____ of A and B is written 'A ∩ B'. Formally:

> x is an element of A ∩ B if and only if
> - x is an element of A and
> - x is an element of B.

For example:
- The _____ of the sets {1, 2, 3} and {2, 3, 4} is {2, 3}.
- The number 9 is not in the _____ of the set of prime numbers {2, 3, 5, 7, 11, …} and the set of odd numbers {1, 3, 5, 7, 9, 11, …}.

If the _____ of two sets A and B is empty, that is they have no elements in common, then they are said to be disjoint, denoted: A ∩ B = Ø. For example the sets {1, 2} and {3, 4} are disjoint, written
{1, 2} ∩ {3, 4} = Ø.

a. Intersection
b. Advice
c. Order
d. Erlang

11. In set theory, the term _____ refers to a set operation used in the convergence of set elements to form a resultant set containing the elements of both sets. As a simple example, a _____ of two disjoint sets, which do not have elements in common results in a set containing all elements from both sets. A Venn diagram representing the _____ of sets A and B.

a. UES
b. Introduction
c. Event
d. Union

12. In simple terms, two events are _____ if they cannot occur at the same time.

In logic, two _____ propositions are propositions that logically cannot both be true. To say that more than two propositions are _____ may, depending on context mean that no two of them can both be true, or only that they cannot all be true.

a. Mutually exclusive
b. Philosophy of mathematics
c. Philosophy
d. Determinism

Chapter 7. PROBABILITY

13. In number theory, a _____ of a positive integer n is a way of writing n as a sum of positive integers. Two sums which only differ in the order of their summands are considered to be the same _____; if order matters then the sum becomes a composition. A summand in a _____ is also called a part.

   a. Congruent
   b. Derivative algebra
   c. Partition
   d. Distribution

14. _____ is the likelihood or chance that something is the case or will happen. Theoretical _____ is used extensively in areas such as statistics, mathematics, science and philosophy to draw conclusions about the likelihood of potential events and the underlying mechanics of complex systems.

   The word _____ does not have a consistent direct definition.

   a. Standardized moment
   b. Discrete random variable
   c. Probability
   d. Statistical significance

15. In statistics the _____ of an event i is the number n_i of times the event occurred in the experiment or the study. These frequencies are often graphically represented in histograms.

   We speak of absolute frequencies, when the counts n_i themselves are given and of

   $$f_i = \frac{n_i}{N} = \frac{n_i}{\sum_i n_i}$$

   Taking the f_i for all i and tabulating or plotting them leads to a _____ distribution.

   a. Subharmonic
   b. Digital room correction
   c. Robinson-Dadson curves
   d. Frequency

16. _____ is the probability of some event A, given the occurrence of some other event B. _____ is written P[A│B], and is read 'the probability of A, given B'.

   Joint probability is the probability of two events in conjunction. That is, it is the probability of both events together. The joint probability of A and B is written $P(A \cap B)$ or $P(A,B)$.

a. Quantile
b. Conditional probability
c. Sample space
d. Renewal theory

17. In operations research, specifically in decision analysis, a _____ is a decision support tool that uses a graph or model of decisions and their possible consequences, including chance event outcomes, resource costs, and utility. A _____ is used to identify the strategy most likely to reach a goal. Another use of trees is as a descriptive means for calculating conditional probabilities.
   a. Decision tree
   b. 2-3 heap
   c. 120-cell
   d. 1-center problem

18. In differential geometry, a discipline within mathematics, a _____ is a subset of the tangent bundle of a manifold satisfying certain properties. _____s are used to build up notions of integrability, and specifically of a foliation of a manifold
   a. Coherence
   b. Constraint
   c. Discontinuity
   d. Distribution

19. In probability theory and statistics, a _____ identifies either the probability of each value of an unidentified random variable, or the probability of the value falling within a particular interval. The probability function describes the range of possible values that a random variable can attain and the probability that the value of the random variable is within any subset of that range.

When the random variable takes values in the set of real numbers, the _____ is completely described by the cumulative distribution function, whose value at each real x is the probability that the random variable is smaller than or equal to x.

   a. Normal distribution
   b. Probability distribution
   c. Statistical graphics
   d. Z-test

Chapter 7. PROBABILITY

20. In set theory, a _____ is a partially ordered set such that for each t ∈ T, the set {s ∈ T : s < t} is well-ordered by the relation <. For each t ∈ T, the order type of {s ∈ T : s < t} is called the height of t. The height of T itself is the least ordinal greater than the height of each element of T.
   a. Transitive reduction
   b. Set-theoretic topology
   c. Definable numbers
   d. Tree

21. In mathematics, a _____ is a way of expressing a number as a fraction of 100. It is often denoted using the percent sign, '%'. For example, 45% is equal to 45 / 100, or 0.45.
   a. Least common multiple
   b. Percentage
   c. Lowest common denominator
   d. Subtrahend

22. In mathematics, the _____ is a direct product of sets. The _____ is named after René Descartes, whose formulation of analytic geometry gave rise to this concept.

   Specifically, the _____ of two sets X and Y, denoted X × Y, is the set of all possible ordered pairs whose first component is a member of X and whose second component is a member of Y:

   $$X \times Y = \{(x,y) | x \in X \text{ and } y \in Y\}.$$

   For example, the _____ of the 13-element set of standard playing card ranks {Ace, King, Queen, Jack, 10, 9, 8, 7, 6, 5, 4, 3, 2} and the four-element set of card suits {â™ , â™¥, â™¦, â™£} is the 52-element set of all possible playing cards ,, …,,, …,,}.

   a. Disjoint sets
   b. Cartesian product
   c. Choice function
   d. Set of all sets

23. In statistics, a _____ is an idealized randomizing device with two states which are equally likely to occur. It is based on the ubiquitous coin flip used in sports and other situations where it is necessary to give two parties the same chance of winning. Depending on the occasion a specially designed chip or a simple currency coin is used, which due to unequal weight distribution might be 'unfair': one state might occur more frequently than the other, giving one party an unfair advantage.

a. Burr distribution
b. Fair coin
c. Medical statistics
d. Count data

24. A _____ is a computational or physical device designed to generate a sequence of numbers or symbols that lack any pattern. Computer-based systems for random number generation are widely used, but often fall short of this goal, though they may meet some statistical tests for randomness intended to ensure that they do not have any easily discernible patterns. Methods for generating random results have existed since ancient times, including dice, coin flipping, the shuffling of playing cards, the use of yarrow stalks in the I Ching, and many other techniques.

a. Constant-weight code
b. Typical set
c. Random number generator
d. Shannon limit

25. The _____ of a statistical sample is the number of observations that constitute it. It is typically denoted n, a positive integer.

Typically, all else being equal, a larger _____ leads to increased precision in estimates of various properties of the population.

a. Poisson regression
b. Standardized moment
c. False positive
d. Sample size

26. _____ are small polyhedral objects, usually cubic, used for generating random numbers or other symbols. This makes _____ suitable as gambling devices, especially for craps or sic bo, or for use in non-gambling tabletop games.

A traditional die is a cube, marked on each of its six faces with a different number of circular patches or pits called pips.

a. Dice
b. 2-3 heap
c. 120-cell
d. 1-center problem

Chapter 7. PROBABILITY

27. _____ involves reducing the number of significant digits in a number. The result of _____ is a 'shorter' number having fewer non-zero digits yet similar in magnitude. The result is less precise but easier to use.
   a. Hyper operator
   b. Shabakh
   c. Sudan function
   d. Rounding

28. In mathematics, the _____ is a term used to describe the number of times one must apply a given operation to an integer before reaching a fixed point.

Usually, this refers to the additive or multiplicative persistence of an integer, which is how often one has to replace the number by the sum or product of its digits until one reaches a single digit. Because the numbers are broken down into their digits, the additive or multiplicative persistence depends on the radix.

   a. Coprime
   b. Lychrel number
   c. Linear congruence theorem
   d. Persistence of a number

29. The _____ Evaluation and Review Technique, commonly abbreviated PERT, is a model for project management designed to analyze and represent the tasks involved in completing a given project.

PERT is a method to analyze the involved tasks in completing a given project, especially the time needed to complete each task, and identifying the minimum time needed to complete the total project.

This model was invented by Booz Allen Hamilton, Inc.

   a. Key server
   b. Battle of the Sexes
   c. Program
   d. Huge

30. A random number generator is a computational or physical device designed to generate a sequence of numbers or symbols that lack any pattern. Computer-based systems for _____ are widely used, but often fall short of this goal, though they may meet some statistical tests for randomness intended to ensure that they do not have any easily discernible patterns. Methods for generating random results have existed since ancient times, including dice, coin flipping, the shuffling of playing cards, the use of yarrow stalks in the I Ching, and many other techniques.

98   Chapter 7. PROBABILITY

   a. Mutual information
   b. Modulo-N code
   c. Random number generation
   d. Hirschman uncertainty

31. A _____ typically refers to a class of handheld calculators that are capable of plotting graphs, solving simultaneous equations, and performing numerous other tasks with variables. Most popular _____s are also programmable, allowing the user to create customized programs, typically for scientific/engineering and education applications. Due to their large displays intended for graphing, they can also accommodate several lines of text and calculations at a time.
   a. Bump mapping
   b. Support vector machines
   c. Genus
   d. Graphing calculator

32. _____ or amortisation is the process of decreasing an amount over a period of time. The word comes from Middle English amortisen to kill, alienate in mortmain, from Anglo-French amorteser, alteration of amortir, from Vulgar Latin admortire to kill, from Latin ad- + mort-, mors death. Particular instances of the term include:

   - _____, the allocation of a lump sum amount to different time periods, particularly for loans and other forms of finance, including related interest or other finance charges.
     o _____ schedule, a table detailing each periodic payment on a loan, as generated by an _____ calculator.
     o Negative _____, an _____ schedule where the loan amount actually increases through not paying the full interest
   - Amortized analysis, analyzing the execution cost of algorithms over a sequence of operations.
   - _____ of capital expenditures of certain assets under accounting rules, particularly intangible assets, in a manner analogous to depreciation.
   - _____

_____ is also used in the context of zoning regulations and describes the time in which a property owner has to relocate when the property's use constitutes a preexisting nonconforming use under zoning regulations.

   - Depreciation

   a. Amortization
   b. Identity
   c. Origin
   d. ISAAC

Chapter 7. PROBABILITY

33. An _____ is a table detailing each periodic payment on a amortizing loan, as generated by an amortization calculator.

While a portion of every payment is applied towards both the interest and the principal balance of the loan, the exact amount applied to principal each time varies. An _____ reveals the specific monetary amount put towards interest, as well as the specific put towards the Principal balance, with each payment.

- a. Accounts receivable
- b. A Mathematical Theory of Communication
- c. A chemical equation
- d. Amortization schedule

34. A _____ is a device for performing mathematical calculations, distinguished from a computer by having a limited problem solving ability and an interface optimized for interactive calculation rather than programming. _____s can be hardware or software, and mechanical or electronic, and are often built into devices such as PDAs or mobile phones.

Modern electronic _____s are generally small, digital, and usually inexpensive.

- a. 2-3 heap
- b. 1-center problem
- c. 120-cell
- d. Calculator

35. The mathematical concept of a _____ expresses the intuitive idea of deterministic dependence between two quantities, one of which is viewed as primary and the other as secondary. A _____ then is a way to associate a unique output for each input of a specified type, for example, a real number or an element of a given set.

- a. Function
- b. Grill
- c. Going up
- d. Coherent

36. _____ is the use of statistics to analyze characteristics or changes to a population. It is related to social demography and demography.

_____ can analyze anything from global demographic changes to local small scale changes.

a. Higher-order statistics
b. Cross-sectional data
c. Population statistics
d. Sequential estimation

37. A _____ is the result of applying a function to a set of data.

More formally, statistical theory defines a _____ as a function of a sample where the function itself is independent of the sample's distribution: the term is used both for the function and for the value of the function on a given sample.

A _____ is distinct from an unknown statistical parameter, which is not computable from a sample.

a. Statistic
b. Parameter space
c. Loss function
d. Spatial dependence

38. _____ is a mathematical science pertaining to the collection, analysis, interpretation or explanation, and presentation of data. It also provides tools for prediction and forecasting based on data. It is applicable to a wide variety of academic disciplines, from the natural and social sciences to the humanities, government and business.
a. Percentile rank
b. Regression toward the mean
c. Statistics
d. Probability distribution

39. In mathematics, computing, linguistics and related subjects, an _____ is a sequence of finite instructions, often used for calculation and data processing. It is formally a type of effective method in which a list of well-defined instructions for completing a task will, when given an initial state, proceed through a well-defined series of successive states, eventually terminating in an end-state. The transition from one state to the next is not necessarily deterministic; some _____s, known as probabilistic _____s, incorporate randomness.
a. Out-of-core
b. Approximate counting algorithm
c. Algorithm
d. In-place algorithm

40. _____ occurs when the identities of two or more individuals, concepts sharing some characteristics of one another, become confused until there seems to be only a single identity.

Chapter 7. PROBABILITY

In language, idiom _____ is the amalgamation of two different expressions. In most cases, the combination results in a new expression that makes little sense literally, but clearly expresses an idea because it references well-known idioms.

a. Finitism
b. Proof theory
c. Validity
d. Conflation

41. In the mathematics of probability, an _____ is an event x with a probability Pr of zero, or Pr(x) = 0.

An _____ is not the same as the stronger concept of logical impossibility. For any continuous probability distribution the probability of any single elementary event is 0, yet the event is not logically impossible as an event outside the distribution.

a. A Mathematical Theory of Communication
b. A posteriori
c. Impossible Event
d. A chemical equation

42. The _____ or Dirac's delta is a mathematical construct introduced by the British theoretical physicist Paul Dirac. Informally, it is a function representing an infinitely sharp peak bounding unit area: a function that has the value zero everywhere except at x = 0 where its value is infinitely large in such a way that its total integral is 1. It is a continuous analogue of the discrete Kronecker delta.

a. Weak derivative
b. Hyperfunction
c. Dirac delta
d. Schwartz kernel theorem

43. In mathematics, and more specifically set theory, the _____ is the unique set having no members. Some axiomatic set theories assure that the _____ exists by including an axiom of _____; in other theories, its existence can be deduced. Many possible properties of sets are trivially true for the _____.

a. Empty function
b. Inverse function
c. A Mathematical Theory of Communication
d. Empty set

Chapter 7. PROBABILITY

44. _____ is the mathematical operation of scaling one number by another. It is one of the four basic operations in elementary arithmetic.

_____ is defined for whole numbers in terms of repeated addition; for example, 4 multiplied by 3 can be calculated by adding 3 copies of 4 together:

$$4 + 4 + 4 = 12.$$

_____ of rational numbers and real numbers is defined by systematic generalization of this basic idea.

   a. Least common multiple
   b. Multiplication
   c. The number 0 is even.
   d. Highest common factor

45. A _____ is a 2D geometric symbolic representation of information according to some visualization technique. Sometimes, the technique uses a 3D visualization which is then projected onto the 2D surface. The word graph is sometimes used as a synonym for _____.
   a. 2-3 heap
   b. Diagram
   c. 1-center problem
   d. 120-cell

46. In mathematics, the _____ of a number n is the number that, when added to n, yields zero. The _____ of n is denoted −n. For example, 7 is −7, because 7 + (−7) = 0, and the _____ of −0.3 is 0.3, because −0.3 + 0.3 = 0.
   a. Additive inverse
   b. Algebraic structure
   c. Arity
   d. Associativity

47. In mathematics, a _____ is a set of real numbers with the property that any number that lies between two numbers in the set is also included in the set. For example, the set of all numbers x satisfying $0 \leq x \leq 1$ is an _____ which contains 0 and 1, as well as all numbers between them. Other examples of _____s are the set of all real numbers $\mathbb{R}$, the set of all positive real numbers, and the empty set.
   a. Interval
   b. Annihilator
   c. Ideal
   d. Order

Chapter 7. PROBABILITY

48. In statistics, the terms Type I error and type II error are used to describe possible errors made in a statistical decision process. In 1928, Jerzy Neyman and Egon Pearson, both eminent statisticians, discussed the problems associated with 'deciding whether or not a particular sample may be judged as likely to have been randomly drawn from a certain population': and identified 'two sources of error', namely:

    null hypothesis, and
    null hypothesis

In 1930, they elaborated on these two sources of error, remarking that 'in testing hypotheses two considerations must be kept in view, we must be able to reduce the chance of rejecting a true hypothesis to as low a value as desired; the test must be so devised that it will reject the hypothesis tested when it is likely to be false'

When an observer makes a Type I error in evaluating a sample against its parent population, s/he is mistakenly thinking that a statistical difference exists when in truth there is no statistical difference. For example, imagine that a pregnancy test has produced a 'positive' result; if the woman is actually not pregnant though, then we say the test produced a '_____'.

    a. Mathematical statistics
    b. Chi-square test
    c. False positive
    d. Covariance

49. In mathematics, a _____ is a statement that can be proved on the basis of explicitly stated or previously agreed assumptions.
    a. Disjunction introduction
    b. Theorem
    c. Boolean function
    d. Logical value

Chapter 8. RANDOM VARIABLES AND STATISTICS

1. In probability theory, an _____ is a set of outcomes to which a probability is assigned. Typically, when the sample space is finite, any subset of the sample space is an _____. However, this approach does not work well in cases where the sample space is infinite, most notably when the outcome is a real number.
   a. Event
   b. Equaliser
   c. Information set
   d. Audio compression

2. In game theory, an _____ is a set of moves or strategies taken by the players, or their payoffs resulting from the actions or strategies taken by all players. The two are complementary in that given knowledge of the set of strategies of all players, the final state of the game is known, as are any relevant payoffs. In a game where chance or a random event is involved, the _____ is not known from only the set of strategies, but is only realized when the random even are realized.
   a. Autonomous system
   b. Algebraic
   c. Equaliser
   d. Outcome

3. In mathematics, _____ are used in the study of chance and probability. They were developed to assist in the analysis of games of chance, stochastic events, and the results of scientific experiments by capturing only the mathematical properties necessary to answer probabilistic questions. Further formalizations have firmly grounded the entity in the theoretical domains of mathematics by making use of measure theory.
   a. Statistics
   b. Statistical dispersion
   c. Median polish
   d. Random variables

4. In statistics, a _____ is a subset of a population. Typically, the population is very large, making a census or a complete enumeration of all the values in the population impractical or impossible. The _____ represents a subset of manageable size.
   a. Sample
   b. Boussinesq approximation
   c. Dispersion
   d. Duality

5. In probability theory, the _____ or universal _____, often denoted S, Ω of an experiment or random trial is the set of all possible outcomes. For example, if the experiment is tossing a coin, the _____ is the set {head, tail}. For tossing a single six-sided die, the _____ is {1, 2, 3, 4, 5, 6}.

a. Markov chain
b. Marginal distribution
c. Martingale central limit theorem
d. Sample space

6. A _____ is the result of applying a function to a set of data.

More formally, statistical theory defines a _____ as a function of a sample where the function itself is independent of the sample's distribution: the term is used both for the function and for the value of the function on a given sample.

A _____ is distinct from an unknown statistical parameter, which is not computable from a sample.

a. Loss function
b. Spatial dependence
c. Parameter space
d. Statistic

7. _____ is a mathematical science pertaining to the collection, analysis, interpretation or explanation, and presentation of data. It also provides tools for prediction and forecasting based on data. It is applicable to a wide variety of academic disciplines, from the natural and social sciences to the humanities, government and business.
a. Percentile rank
b. Regression toward the mean
c. Statistics
d. Probability distribution

8. In elementary algebra, a _____ is a polynomial with two terms: the sum of two monomials. It is the simplest kind of polynomial except for a monomial.

The _____ $a^2 - b^2$ can be factored as the product of two other _____ s:

$a^2 - b^2$.

The product of a pair of linear _____ s a x + b and c x + d is:

2 +x + bd.

Chapter 8. RANDOM VARIABLES AND STATISTICS

A _____ raised to the nth power, represented as

n

can be expanded by means of the _____ theorem or, equivalently, using Pascal's triangle.

a. Cylindrical algebraic decomposition
b. Rational root theorem
c. Binomial
d. Real structure

9. In mathematics, _____ and undefined are used to explain whether or not expressions have meaningful, sensible, and unambiguous values. Not all branches of mathematics come to the same conclusion.

The following expressions are undefined in all contexts, but remarks in the analysis section may apply.

a. Plugging in
b. LHS
c. Toy model
d. Defined

10. In number theory, a _____ of a positive integer n is a way of writing n as a sum of positive integers. Two sums which only differ in the order of their summands are considered to be the same _____; if order matters then the sum becomes a composition. A summand in a _____ is also called a part.

a. Distribution
b. Congruent
c. Derivative algebra
d. Partition

11. In probability theory, a probability distribution is called _____ if its cumulative distribution function is _____. That is equivalent to saying that for random variables X with the distribution in question, Pr[X = a] = 0 for all real numbers a. If the distribution of X is _____ then X is called a _____ random variable.

a. Conull set
b. Concatenated codes
c. Continuous phase modulation
d. Continuous

Chapter 8. RANDOM VARIABLES AND STATISTICS

12. In probability theory, a probability distribution is called discrete if it is characterized by a probability mass function. Thus, the distribution of a random variable X is discrete, and X is then called a _____, if

$$\sum_u \Pr(X = u) = 1$$

as u runs through the set of all possible values of X.

If a random variable is discrete, then the set of all values that it can assume with non-zero probability is finite or countably infinite, because the sum of uncountably many positive real numbers always diverges to infinity.

a. Regression toward the mean
b. Statistics
c. First-hitting-time models
d. Discrete random variable

13. _____ is the probability of some event A, given the occurrence of some other event B. _____ is written P[A | B], and is read 'the probability of A, given B'.

Joint probability is the probability of two events in conjunction. That is, it is the probability of both events together. The joint probability of A and B is written $P(A \cap B)$ or $P(A.B)$.

a. Quantile
b. Sample space
c. Renewal theory
d. Conditional probability

14. _____ typically deals with the probability of several successive decisions, each of which has two possible outcomes.

The probability of an event can be expressed as a _____ if its outcomes can be broken down into two probabilities p and q, where p and q are complementary For example, tossing a coin can be either heads or tails, each which have a probability of 0.5. Rolling a four on a six-sided die can be expressed as the probability of getting a 4 or the probability of rolling something else.

a. Binomial probability
b. Marginal distribution
c. Quantile
d. Markov chain

Chapter 8. RANDOM VARIABLES AND STATISTICS

15. In differential geometry, a discipline within mathematics, a _____ is a subset of the tangent bundle of a manifold satisfying certain properties. _____s are used to build up notions of integrability, and specifically of a foliation of a manifold
    a. Constraint
    b. Coherence
    c. Discontinuity
    d. Distribution

16. _____ is the likelihood or chance that something is the case or will happen. Theoretical _____ is used extensively in areas such as statistics, mathematics, science and philosophy to draw conclusions about the likelihood of potential events and the underlying mechanics of complex systems.

    The word _____ does not have a consistent direct definition.

    a. Discrete random variable
    b. Statistical significance
    c. Standardized moment
    d. Probability

17. In probability theory and statistics, a _____ identifies either the probability of each value of an unidentified random variable, or the probability of the value falling within a particular interval. The probability function describes the range of possible values that a random variable can attain and the probability that the value of the random variable is within any subset of that range.

    When the random variable takes values in the set of real numbers, the _____ is completely described by the cumulative distribution function, whose value at each real x is the probability that the random variable is smaller than or equal to x.

    a. Normal distribution
    b. Z-test
    c. Statistical graphics
    d. Probability distribution

18. In statistics the _____ of an event i is the number n_i of times the event occurred in the experiment or the study. These frequencies are often graphically represented in histograms.

    We speak of absolute frequencies, when the counts n_i themselves are given and of

$$f_i = \frac{n_i}{N} = \frac{n_i}{\sum_i n_i}$$

Taking the f₁ for all i and tabulating or plotting them leads to a _____ distribution.

a. Subharmonic
b. Frequency
c. Robinson-Dadson curves
d. Digital room correction

19. In statistics, a _____ is a list of the values that a variable takes in a sample. It is usually a list, ordered by quantity, showing the number of times each value appears. For example, if 100 people rate a five-point Likert scale assessing their agreement with a statement on a scale on which 1 denotes strong agreement and 5 strong disagreement, the _____ of their responses might look like:

This simple tabulation has two drawbacks.

a. Covariance
b. Confounding
c. Frequency distribution
d. Percentile

20. The framework of quantum mechanics requires a careful definition of _____, and a thorough discussion of its practical and philosophical implications.

_____ is viewed in different ways in the many interpretations of quantum mechanics; however, despite the considerable philosophical differences, they almost universally agree on the practical question of what results from a routine quantum-physics laboratory _____. To describe this, a simple framework to use is the Copenhagen interpretation, and it will be implicitly used in this section; the utility of this approach has been verified countless times, and all other interpretations are necessarily constructed so as to give the same quantitative predictions as this in almost every case.

a. 1-center problem
b. Measurement
c. Dynamic range
d. Fundamental units

Chapter 8. RANDOM VARIABLES AND STATISTICS

21. In set theory and its applications throughout mathematics, a _____ is a collection of sets that can be unambiguously defined by a property that all its members share. The precise definition of '_____' depends on foundational context. In work on ZF set theory, the notion of _____ is informal, whereas other set theories, such as NBG set theory, axiomatize the notion of '_____'.
    a. Filter
    b. Class
    c. Coherence
    d. Congruent

22. In mathematics, the _____ is a direct product of sets. The _____ is named after René Descartes, whose formulation of analytic geometry gave rise to this concept.

    Specifically, the _____ of two sets X and Y, denoted X × Y, is the set of all possible ordered pairs whose first component is a member of X and whose second component is a member of Y:

    $$X \times Y = \{(x,y) | x \in X \text{ and } y \in Y\}.$$

    For example, the _____ of the 13-element set of standard playing card ranks {Ace, King, Queen, Jack, 10, 9, 8, 7, 6, 5, 4, 3, 2} and the four-element set of card suits {â™ , â™¥, â™¦, â™£} is the 52-element set of all possible playing cards ,, ...,,, ...,}.

    a. Choice function
    b. Cartesian product
    c. Disjoint sets
    d. Set of all sets

23. A _____ typically refers to a class of handheld calculators that are capable of plotting graphs, solving simultaneous equations, and performing numerous other tasks with variables. Most popular _____s are also programmable, allowing the user to create customized programs, typically for scientific/engineering and education applications. Due to their large displays intended for graphing, they can also accommodate several lines of text and calculations at a time.
    a. Genus
    b. Bump mapping
    c. Support vector machines
    d. Graphing calculator

Chapter 8. RANDOM VARIABLES AND STATISTICS

24. _____ or amortisation is the process of decreasing an amount over a period of time. The word comes from Middle English amortisen to kill, alienate in mortmain, from Anglo-French amorteser, alteration of amortir, from Vulgar Latin admortire to kill, from Latin ad- + mort-, mors death. Particular instances of the term include:

- _____, the allocation of a lump sum amount to different time periods, particularly for loans and other forms of finance, including related interest or other finance charges.
  - _____ schedule, a table detailing each periodic payment on a loan, as generated by an _____ calculator.
  - Negative _____, an _____ schedule where the loan amount actually increases through not paying the full interest
- Amortized analysis, analyzing the execution cost of algorithms over a sequence of operations.
- _____ of capital expenditures of certain assets under accounting rules, particularly intangible assets, in a manner analogous to depreciation.
- _____

_____ is also used in the context of zoning regulations and describes the time in which a property owner has to relocate when the property's use constitutes a preexisting nonconforming use under zoning regulations.

- Depreciation

a. Identity
b. Origin
c. ISAAC
d. Amortization

25. An _____ is a table detailing each periodic payment on a amortizing loan, as generated by an amortization calculator.

While a portion of every payment is applied towards both the interest and the principal balance of the loan, the exact amount applied to principal each time varies. An _____ reveals the specific monetary amount put towards interest, as well as the specific put towards the Principal balance, with each payment.

a. Amortization schedule
b. Accounts receivable
c. A chemical equation
d. A Mathematical Theory of Communication

26. A _____ is a device for performing mathematical calculations, distinguished from a computer by having a limited problem solving ability and an interface optimized for interactive calculation rather than programming. _____s can be hardware or software, and mechanical or electronic, and are often built into devices such as PDAs or mobile phones.

Modern electronic _____s are generally small, digital, and usually inexpensive.

a. 2-3 heap
b. 120-cell
c. 1-center problem
d. Calculator

27. In statistics, a _____ is a graphical display of tabulated frequencies, shown as bars. It shows what proportion of cases fall into each of several categories. A _____ differs from a bar chart in that it is the area of the bar that denotes the value, not the height as in bar charts, a crucial distinction when the categories are not of uniform width.

a. Probability distribution
b. Histogram
c. First-hitting-time models
d. Standardized moment

28. Introduction

In the theory of probability and statistics, a _____ is an experiment whose outcome is random and can be either of two possible outcomes, 'success' and 'failure'.

In practice it refers to a single experiment which can have one of two possible outcomes. These events can be phrased into 'yes or no' questions:

- Did the coin land heads?
- Was the newborn child a girl?
- Were a person's eyes green?
- Did a mosquito die after the area was sprayed with insecticide?
- Did a potential customer decide to buy a product?
- Did a citizen vote for a specific candidate?
- Did an employee vote pro-union?

Therefore success and failure are labels for outcomes, and should not be construed literally. Examples of _____s include

- Flipping a coin. In this context, obverse conventionally denotes success and reverse denotes failure. A fair coin has the probability of success 0.5 by definition.
- Rolling a die, where a six is 'success' and everything else a 'failure'.
- In conducting a political opinion poll, choosing a voter at random to ascertain whether that voter will vote 'yes' in an upcoming referendum.

Mathematically, a _____ can be described by a sample space Ω consisting of two values, s for 'success' and f for 'failure'. Therefore the sample space is $\Omega = \{s, f\}$.

   a. Bernoulli trial
   b. Law of total cumulance
   c. Point process
   d. Marginal distribution

29. In probability theory and statistics, the _____ is the discrete probability distribution of the number of successes in a sequence of n independent yes/no experiments, each of which yields success with probability p. Such a success/failure experiment is also called a Bernoulli experiment or Bernoulli trial. In fact, when n = 1, the _____ is a Bernoulli distribution.

   a. Coefficient of variation
   b. Biostatistics
   c. Median
   d. Binomial distribution

30. In scientific inquiry, an _____ is a method of investigating particular types of research questions or solving particular types of problems. The _____ is a cornerstone in the empirical approach to acquiring deeper knowledge about the world and is used in both natural sciences as well as in social sciences. An _____ is defined, in science, as a method of investigating less known fields, solving practical problems and proving theoretical assumptions.

   a. A chemical equation
   b. A posteriori
   c. A Mathematical Theory of Communication
   d. Experiment

31. The mathematical concept of a _____ expresses the intuitive idea of deterministic dependence between two quantities, one of which is viewed as primary and the other as secondary. A _____ then is a way to associate a unique output for each input of a specified type, for example, a real number or an element of a given set.

   a. Going up
   b. Coherent
   c. Grill
   d. Function

32. _____ is an economics theory, that refers to individuals or societies gaining the maximum amount out of the resources they have available to them. The theory proposed by most economists is that _____ refers to the _____ of profit.

As some economists have begun to find out, this theory does not hold true for all people and cultures.

a. Composite
b. Boundary
c. Homogeneity
d. Maximization

33. _____ and sample covariance are statistics computed from a collection of data, thought of as being random.

Given a random sample $X_1, \ldots, X_N$ from an n-dimensional random variable X, the _____ is

$$\bar{X} = \frac{1}{N} \sum_{k=1}^{N} X_k.$$

In coordinates, writing the vectors as columns,

$$X_k = \begin{bmatrix} x_{1k} \\ \vdots \\ x_{nk} \end{bmatrix}, \quad \bar{X} = \begin{bmatrix} \bar{x}_1 \\ \vdots \\ \bar{x}_n \end{bmatrix},$$

the entries of the _____ are

$$\bar{x}_i = \frac{1}{N} \sum_{k=1}^{N} x_{ik}, \quad i = 1, \ldots, n.$$

The sample covariance of $X_1, \ldots, X_N$ is the n-by-n matrix $Q = [q_{ij}]$ with the entries given by

$$q_{ij} = \frac{1}{N-1} \sum_{k=1}^{N} (x_{ik} - \bar{x}_i)(x_{jk} - \bar{x}_j)$$

The _____ and the sample covariance matrix are unbiased estimates of the mean and the covariance matrix of the random variable X. The reason why the sample covariance matrix has $N-1$ in the denominator rather than N is essentially that the population mean E is not known and is replaced by the _____ $\bar{x}$.

a. Covariance
b. Mathematical statistics
c. Skewness
d. Sample mean

34. In signal processing, _____ is the reduction of a continuous signal to a discrete signal. A common example is the conversion of a sound wave to a sequence of samples.

A sample refers to a value or set of values at a point in time and/or space.

a. Converse logic
b. Decidable
c. Disk
d. Sampling

35. In statistics, the _____ or _____ function is the partial derivative, with respect to some parameter θ, of the logarithm of the likelihood function. If the observation is X and its likelihood is L, then the _____ V can be found through the chain rule:

$$V = \frac{\partial}{\partial \theta} \log L(\theta; X) = \frac{1}{L(\theta; X)} \frac{\partial L(\theta; X)}{\partial \theta}.$$

Note that V is a function of θ and the observation X, so that, in general, it is not a statistic. Note also that V indicates the sensitivity of L.

a. Deviation
b. Functional
c. Cleaver
d. Score

36. _____ is the addition of a set of numbers; the result is their sum or total. An interim or present total of a _____ process is termed the running total. The 'numbers' to be summed may be natural numbers, complex numbers, matrices, or still more complicated objects.

a. 120-cell
b. 2-3 heap
c. 1-center problem
d. Summation

Chapter 8. RANDOM VARIABLES AND STATISTICS

37. In statistics, _____ has two related meanings:

   - the arithmetic _____.
   - the expected value of a random variable, which is also called the population _____.

   It is sometimes stated that the '_____' _____s average. This is incorrect if '_____' is taken in the specific sense of 'arithmetic _____' as there are different types of averages: the _____, median, and mode. For instance, average house prices almost always use the median value for the average.

   For a real-valued random variable X, the _____ is the expectation of X.

   a. Proportional hazards model
   b. Statistical population
   c. Probability
   d. Mean

38. In mathematics the concept of a _____ generalizes notions such as 'length', 'area', and 'volume'. Informally, given some base set, a '_____' is any consistent assignment of 'sizes' to the subsets of the base set. Depending on the application, the 'size' of a subset may be interpreted as its physical size, the amount of something that lies within the subset, or the probability that some random process will yield a result within the subset.
   a. Cusp
   b. Congruent
   c. Lattice
   d. Measure

39. In statistics, the _____ is the value that occurs the most frequently in a data set or a probability distribution. In some fields, notably education, sample data are often called scores, and the sample _____ is known as the modal score.

   Like the statistical mean and the median, the _____ is a way of capturing important information about a random variable or a population in a single quantity.

   a. Deltoid
   b. Function
   c. Field
   d. Mode

40. The _____ of a statistical sample is the number of observations that constitute it. It is typically denoted n, a positive integer.

Chapter 8. RANDOM VARIABLES AND STATISTICS

Typically, all else being equal, a larger _____ leads to increased precision in estimates of various properties of the population.

a. Standardized moment
b. Poisson regression
c. False positive
d. Sample size

41. In mathematics, an average, or _____ of a data set refers to a measure of the 'middle' or 'expected' value of the data set. There are many different descriptive statistics that can be chosen as a measurement of the _____ of the data items.

An average is a single value that is meant to typify a list of values.

a. Trimean
b. Quartile
c. Central tendency
d. Mean reciprocal rank

42. In probability theory and statistics, the _____ of a random variable is the integral of the random variable with respect to its probability measure. For discrete random variables this is equivalent to the probability-weighted sum of the possible values, and for continuous random variables with a density function it is the probability density -weighted integral of the possible values.

The _____ may be intuitively understood by the law of large numbers: The _____, when it exists, is almost surely the limit of the sample mean as sample size grows to infinity.

a. Illustration
b. Infinitely divisible distribution
c. Event
d. Expected value

43. In mathematics, the _____ is an important formula giving the expansion of powers of sums. Its simplest version states that

$$(x+y)^n = \sum_{k=0}^{n} \binom{n}{k} x^{n-k} y^k \qquad (1)$$

for any real or complex numbers x and y, and any nonnegative integer n. The binomial coefficient appearing in may be defined in terms of the factorial function n!:

$$\binom{n}{k} = \frac{n!}{k!\,(n-k)!}.$$

For example, here are the cases where $2 \leq n \leq 5$:

$$(x+y)^2 = x^2 + 2xy + y^2$$
$$(x+y)^3 = x^3 + 3x^2y + 3xy^2 + y^3$$
$$(x+y)^4 = x^4 + 4x^3y + 6x^2y^2 + 4xy^3 + y^4$$
$$(x+y)^5 = x^5 + 5x^4y + 10x^3y^2 + 10x^2y^3 + 5xy^4 + y^5.$$

Formula is valid more generally for any elements x and y of a semiring as long as xy = yx..

a. Hypergeometric identities
b. Binomial theorem
c. Lah numbers
d. Stirling transform

44. A _____ is a structured activity, usually undertaken for enjoyment and sometimes also used as an educational tool. _____s are distinct from work, which is usually carried out for remuneration, and from art, which is more concerned with the expression of ideas. However, the distinction is not clear-cut, and many _____s are also considered to be work (such as professional players of spectator sports/_____s) or art (such as jigsaw puzzles or _____s involving an artistic layout such as Mah-jongg solitaire.)

a. 120-cell
b. 2-3 heap
c. 1-center problem
d. Game

45. In mathematics, a _____ is a statement that can be proved on the basis of explicitly stated or previously agreed assumptions.

a. Logical value
b. Boolean function
c. Disjunction introduction
d. Theorem

Chapter 8. RANDOM VARIABLES AND STATISTICS

46. In probability and statistics, the _____ is a measure of the dispersion of a collection of numbers. It can apply to a probability distribution, a random variable, a population or a data set. The _____ is usually denoted with the letter σ.
   a. Standard deviation
   b. Failure rate
   c. Null hypothesis
   d. Statistical population

47. In probability theory and statistics, the _____ of a random variable, probability distribution averaging the squared distance of its possible values from the expected value. Whereas the mean is a way to describe the location of a distribution, the _____ is a way to capture its scale or degree of being spread out. The unit of _____ is the square of the unit of the original variable.
   a. Kendall tau rank correlation coefficient
   b. Variance
   c. Nonlinear regression
   d. Probability distribution

48. In mathematics and statistics, _____ is a measure of difference for interval and ratio variables between the observed value and the mean. The sign of _____, either positive or negative, indicates whether the observation is larger than or smaller than the mean. The magnitude of the value reports how different an observation is from the mean.
   a. Filter
   b. Conchoid
   c. Functional
   d. Deviation

49. The _____ Evaluation and Review Technique, commonly abbreviated PERT, is a model for project management designed to analyze and represent the tasks involved in completing a given project.

PERT is a method to analyze the involved tasks in completing a given project, especially the time needed to complete each task, and identifying the minimum time needed to complete the total project.

This model was invented by Booz Allen Hamilton, Inc.

   a. Battle of the Sexes
   b. Huge
   c. Program
   d. Key server

Chapter 8. RANDOM VARIABLES AND STATISTICS

50. The word _____ denotes information gained by means of observation, experience as opposed to theoretical. A central concept in science and the scientific method is that all evidence must be _____ that is, dependent on evidence or consequences that are observable by the senses. It is usually differentiated from the philosophic usage of empiricism by the use of the adjective '_____' or the adverb 'empirically.' '_____' as an adjective or adverb is used in conjunction with both the natural and social sciences, and refers to the use of working hypotheses that are testable using observation or experiment.

   a. A posteriori
   b. A Mathematical Theory of Communication
   c. A chemical equation
   d. Empirical

51. In mathematics, specifically in combinatorial commutative algebra, a convex lattice polytope P is called _____ if it has the following property: given any positive integer n, every lattice point of the dilation nP, obtained from P by scaling its vertices by the factor n and taking the convex hull of the resulting points, can be written as the sum of exactly n lattice points in P. This property plays an important role in the theory of toric varieties, where it corresponds to projective normality of the toric variety determined by P.

The simplex in R^k with the vertices at the origin and along the unit coordinate vectors is _____.

   a. Polytetrahedron
   b. Hypercube
   c. Normal
   d. Demihypercubes

52. In mathematics, a _____ is a function that represents a probability distribution in terms of integrals.

Formally, a probability distribution has density f, if f is a non-negative Lebesgue-integrable function $\mathbb{R} \to \mathbb{R}$ such that the probability of the interval [a, b] is given by

$$\int_a^b f(x)\,dx$$

for any two numbers a and b. This implies that the total integral of f must be 1.

   a. Law of total variance
   b. Quantile
   c. Probability density function
   d. Pseudocount

Chapter 8. RANDOM VARIABLES AND STATISTICS

53. The _____ of a material is defined as its mass per unit volume:

$$\rho = \frac{m}{V}$$

Different materials usually have different densities, so _____ is an important concept regarding buoyancy, metal purity and packaging.

In some cases _____ is expressed as the dimensionless quantities specific gravity or relative _____, in which case it is expressed in multiples of the _____ of some other standard material, usually water or air.

In a well-known story, Archimedes was given the task of determining whether King Hiero's goldsmith was embezzling gold during the manufacture of a wreath dedicated to the gods and replacing it with another, cheaper alloy.

   a. 120-cell
   b. 2-3 heap
   c. Density
   d. 1-center problem

54. In differential calculus, an _____, or point of inflection is a point on a curve at which the curvature changes sign. The curve changes from being concave upwards to concave downwards, or vice versa. If one imagines driving a vehicle along the curve, it is a point at which the steering-wheel is momentarily 'straight', being turned from left to right or vice versa.
   a. Ordinary differential equation
   b. Implicit function
   c. Implicit differentiation
   d. Inflection point

55. The _____ is an important family of continuous probability distributions, applicable in many fields. Each member of the family may be defined by two parameters, location and scale: the mean and variance respectively. The standard _____ is the _____ with a mean of zero and a variance of one.
   a. Coefficient of variation
   b. Percentile rank
   c. Null hypothesis
   d. Normal distribution

56. where Y is a normally distributed random variable with the same expected value and the same variance as X. This addition of 1/2 to x is a _____.

A _____ can also be applied when other discrete distributions supported on the integers are approximated by the normal distribution.

a. Continuous
b. Convex polygon
c. Coordinate-free treatment
d. Continuity correction

57. _____ In statistics, a result is called statistically significant if it is unlikely to have occurred by chance. "A statistically significant difference" simply means there is statistical evidence that there is a difference; it does not mean the difference is necessarily large, important, or significant in the common meaning of the word.

a. Confounding
b. Variance
c. Survival analysis
d. Statistical significance

58. In mathematics, the _____ is a term used to describe the number of times one must apply a given operation to an integer before reaching a fixed point.

Usually, this refers to the additive or multiplicative persistence of an integer, which is how often one has to replace the number by the sum or product of its digits until one reaches a single digit. Because the numbers are broken down into their digits, the additive or multiplicative persistence depends on the radix.

a. Lychrel number
b. Linear congruence theorem
c. Coprime
d. Persistence of a number

59. In probability theory and statistics, the _____ is one of the most widely used theoretical probability distributions in inferential statistics, e.g., in statistical significance tests. It is useful because, under reasonable assumptions, easily calculated quantities can be proven to have distributions that approximate to the _____ if the null hypothesis is true.

The best-known situations in which the _____ are used are the common chi-square tests for goodness of fit of an observed distribution to a theoretical one, and of the independence of two criteria of classification of qualitative data.

a. Survival analysis
b. Failure rate
c. Sampling distribution
d. Chi-square distribution

60. _____ is a general term used in explaining dependence on parameters, and implying the possibility of counting the number of those parameters. In mathematical terms, the _____ are the dimensions of a phase space.

In mechanics, for each particle belonging to a system, and for each independent direction in which movement is possible, two _____ are defined, one describing the particle's momentum in that direction, the other describing the particle's position along an axis defined by that direction.

a. Character
b. Battle of the Sexes
c. Decidable
d. Degrees of freedom

Chapter 9. MARKOV SYSTEMS

1. In computational complexity theory, an algorithm is said to take _____ if the asymptotic upper bound for the time it requires is proportional to the size of the input, which is usually denoted n.

Informally spoken, the running time increases linearly with the size of the input. For example, a procedure that adds up all elements of a list requires time proportional to the length of the list.

   a. Time-constructible function
   b. Constructible function
   c. Linear time
   d. Truth table reduction

2. In automata theory and sequential logic, a _____ table is a table showing what state a finite semiautomaton or finite state machine will move to, based on the current state and other inputs. A state table is essentially a truth table in which some of the inputs are the current state, and the outputs include the next state, along with other outputs.

A state table is one of many ways to specify a state machine, other ways being a state diagram, and a characteristic equation.

   a. 2-3 heap
   b. 120-cell
   c. 1-center problem
   d. State transition

3. In mathematics, a _____, named after Andrey Markov, is a stochastic process with the Markov property. Having the Markov property means that, given the present state, future states are independent of the past states. In other words, the description of the present state fully captures all the information that could influence the future evolution of the process. Future states will be reached through a probabilistic process instead of a deterministic one.
   a. Possibility theory
   b. Variance-to-mean ratio
   c. Law of Truly Large Numbers
   d. Markov chain

4. A _____ is a 2D geometric symbolic representation of information according to some visualization technique. Sometimes, the technique uses a 3D visualization which is then projected onto the 2D surface. The word graph is sometimes used as a synonym for _____.
   a. Diagram
   b. 120-cell
   c. 2-3 heap
   d. 1-center problem

Chapter 9. MARKOV SYSTEMS

5. In mathematics, a stochastic matrix, probability matrix, or _____ is used to describe the transitions of a Markov chain. It has found use in probability theory, statistics and linear algebra, as well as computer science. There are several different definitions and types of stochastic matrices;

   A right stochastic matrix is a square matrix each of whose rows consists of nonnegative real numbers, with each row summing to 1.

   a. Sylvester matrix
   b. Pick matrix
   c. Hessenberg matrix
   d. Transition matrix

6. In mathematics, a _____ is a rectangular table of elements, which may be numbers or, more generally, any abstract quantities that can be added and multiplied. Matrices are used to describe linear equations, keep track of the coefficients of linear transformations and to record data that depend on multiple parameters. Matrices are described by the field of _____ theory.
   a. Double counting
   b. Coherent
   c. Compression
   d. Matrix

7. A _____, sometimes denoted RW, is a mathematical formalization of a trajectory that consists of taking successive random steps. The results of _____ analysis have been applied to computer science, physics, ecology, economics and a number of other fields as a fundamental model for random processes in time. For example, the path traced by a molecule as it travels in a liquid or a gas, the search path of a foraging animal, the price of a fluctuating stock and the financial status of a gambler can all be modeled as _____ s.
   a. Vector spaces
   b. Bose-Einstein statistics
   c. Phase transition
   d. Random walk

8. Walking is the main form of animal locomotion on land, distinguished from running and crawling. When carried out in shallow waters, it is usually described as wading and when performed over a steeply rising object or an obstacle it becomes scrambling or climbing. The word _____ is descended from the Old English wealcan 'to roll'.
   a. 2-3 heap
   b. Walk
   c. 1-center problem
   d. 120-cell

9. In differential geometry, a discipline within mathematics, a _____ is a subset of the tangent bundle of a manifold satisfying certain properties. _____s are used to build up notions of integrability, and specifically of a foliation of a manifold
   a. Coherence
   b. Discontinuity
   c. Constraint
   d. Distribution

10. Initial objects are also called _____, and terminal objects are also called final.
    a. Direct limit
    b. Terminal object
    c. Colimit
    d. Coterminal

11. In physics and in _____ calculus, a _____ is a concept characterized by a magnitude and a direction. A _____ can be thought of as an arrow in Euclidean space, drawn from an initial point A pointing to a terminal point B.
    a. Deviation
    b. Dominance
    c. Constraint
    d. Vector

12. In mathematics, the _____ is a direct product of sets. The _____ is named after René Descartes, whose formulation of analytic geometry gave rise to this concept.

Specifically, the _____ of two sets X and Y, denoted X × Y, is the set of all possible ordered pairs whose first component is a member of X and whose second component is a member of Y:

$$X \times Y = \{(x,y) | x \in X \text{ and } y \in Y\}.$$

For example, the _____ of the 13-element set of standard playing card ranks {Ace, King, Queen, Jack, 10, 9, 8, 7, 6, 5, 4, 3, 2} and the four-element set of card suits {♠, ♥, ♦, ♣} is the 52-element set of all possible playing cards ,, ...,,, ...,,}.

   a. Cartesian product
   b. Disjoint sets
   c. Set of all sets
   d. Choice function

Chapter 9. MARKOV SYSTEMS

13. A _____ typically refers to a class of handheld calculators that are capable of plotting graphs, solving simultaneous equations, and performing numerous other tasks with variables. Most popular _____s are also programmable, allowing the user to create customized programs, typically for scientific/engineering and education applications. Due to their large displays intended for graphing, they can also accommodate several lines of text and calculations at a time.
    a. Bump mapping
    b. Support vector machines
    c. Genus
    d. Graphing calculator

14. _____ or amortisation is the process of decreasing an amount over a period of time. The word comes from Middle English amortisen to kill, alienate in mortmain, from Anglo-French amorteser, alteration of amortir, from Vulgar Latin admortire to kill, from Latin ad- + mort-, mors death. Particular instances of the term include:

    - _____, the allocation of a lump sum amount to different time periods, particularly for loans and other forms of finance, including related interest or other finance charges.
        o _____ schedule, a table detailing each periodic payment on a loan, as generated by an _____ calculator.
        o Negative _____, an _____ schedule where the loan amount actually increases through not paying the full interest
    - Amortized analysis, analyzing the execution cost of algorithms over a sequence of operations.
    - _____ of capital expenditures of certain assets under accounting rules, particularly intangible assets, in a manner analogous to depreciation.
    - _____

_____ is also used in the context of zoning regulations and describes the time in which a property owner has to relocate when the property's use constitutes a preexisting nonconforming use under zoning regulations.

    - Depreciation

    a. ISAAC
    b. Origin
    c. Identity
    d. Amortization

15. An _____ is a table detailing each periodic payment on a amortizing loan, as generated by an amortization calculator.

While a portion of every payment is applied towards both the interest and the principal balance of the loan, the exact amount applied to principal each time varies. An _____ reveals the specific monetary amount put towards interest, as well as the specific put towards the Principal balance, with each payment.

a. A chemical equation
b. A Mathematical Theory of Communication
c. Accounts receivable
d. Amortization schedule

16. A _____ is a device for performing mathematical calculations, distinguished from a computer by having a limited problem solving ability and an interface optimized for interactive calculation rather than programming. _____s can be hardware or software, and mechanical or electronic, and are often built into devices such as PDAs or mobile phones.

Modern electronic _____s are generally small, digital, and usually inexpensive.

a. 2-3 heap
b. 1-center problem
c. Calculator
d. 120-cell

17. In mathematics, _____ is one of the basic operations defining a vector space in linear algebra. Note that _____ is different from scalar product which is an inner product between two vectors.

More specifically, if K is a field and V is a vector space over K, then _____ is a function from K × V to V.

a. Non-negative matrix factorization
b. Frobenius normal form
c. Jordan normal form
d. Scalar multiplication

18. _____ is the likelihood or chance that something is the case or will happen. Theoretical _____ is used extensively in areas such as statistics, mathematics, science and philosophy to draw conclusions about the likelihood of potential events and the underlying mechanics of complex systems.

The word _____ does not have a consistent direct definition.

a. Statistical significance
b. Standardized moment
c. Discrete random variable
d. Probability

Chapter 9. MARKOV SYSTEMS

19. _____ is the philosophical proposition that every event, including human cognition and behavior, decision and action, is causally determined by an unbroken chain of prior occurrences. With numerous historical debates, many varieties and philosophical positions on the subject of _____ exist from traditions throughout the world.

It is a popular misconception that _____ necessarily entails that humanity or individual humans have no influence on the future and its events; however, determinists believe that the level to which human beings have influence over their future is itself dependent on present and past.

   a. Philosophy
   b. Philosophy of mathematics
   c. Mutually exclusive
   d. Determinism

20. A _____, named after the Russian mathematician Andrey Markov, is a mathematical model for the random evolution of a memoryless system, that is, one for which the likelihood of a given future state, at any given moment, depends only on its present state, and not on any past states.

In a common description, a stochastic process with the Markov property, or memorylessness, is one for which conditional on the present state of the system, its future and past are independent.

Often, the term Markov chain is used to mean a discrete-time _____.

   a. Polar distribution
   b. Hellinger distance
   c. Random measure
   d. Markov process

21. The _____ fallacy is an informal fallacy. It ascribes cause where none exists. The flaw is failing to account for natural fluctuations.
   a. Differential
   b. Depth
   c. Regression
   d. Degrees of freedom

22. The _____ Evaluation and Review Technique, commonly abbreviated PERT, is a model for project management designed to analyze and represent the tasks involved in completing a given project.

PERT is a method to analyze the involved tasks in completing a given project, especially the time needed to complete each task, and identifying the minimum time needed to complete the total project.

Chapter 9. MARKOV SYSTEMS

This model was invented by Booz Allen Hamilton, Inc.

a. Key server
b. Battle of the Sexes
c. Huge
d. Program

23. A _____ is an abstract model that uses mathematical language to describe the behavior of a system. Eykhoff defined a _____ as 'a representation of the essential aspects of an existing system which presents knowledge of that system in usable form'.

a. Metaheuristic
b. Rata Die
c. Total least squares
d. Mathematical model

ANSWER KEY

Chapter 1
1. d	2. b	3. d	4. b	5. d	6. d	7. d	8. b	9. a	10. d
11. d	12. d	13. d	14. c	15. d	16. d	17. d	18. d	19. d	20. d
21. c	22. d	23. b	24. c	25. d	26. d	27. d	28. a	29. d	30. c
31. d	32. c	33. d	34. b	35. a	36. d	37. d	38. d	39. c	40. c
41. d	42. d	43. d	44. a	45. d	46. d	47. d	48. d	49. d	50. b
51. b	52. a	53. d	54. c	55. a	56. a	57. d			

Chapter 2
1. d	2. d	3. d	4. a	5. a	6. b	7. d	8. d	9. d	10. d
11. b	12. d	13. d	14. d	15. c	16. c	17. d	18. b	19. b	20. d
21. a	22. a	23. a	24. a	25. b	26. a	27. a	28. a	29. d	30. b
31. a	32. d	33. d	34. d	35. c					

Chapter 3
1. b	2. b	3. d	4. d	5. a	6. a	7. c	8. d	9. d	10. d
11. d	12. d	13. d	14. d	15. d	16. a	17. b	18. b	19. b	20. d
21. b	22. d	23. a	24. d	25. d	26. d	27. c	28. c	29. d	30. a
31. c	32. c	33. c	34. b	35. c	36. a	37. d	38. d		

Chapter 4
1. d	2. b	3. d	4. d	5. c	6. d	7. c	8. a	9. d	10. a
11. d	12. d	13. a	14. d	15. d	16. d	17. d	18. d	19. d	20. d
21. d	22. b	23. d	24. c	25. b	26. d	27. d	28. a	29. d	30. d
31. c	32. d	33. d	34. d	35. d	36. b	37. a	38. a	39. d	40. d
41. a	42. d	43. b	44. d	45. d	46. d				

Chapter 5
1. c	2. c	3. d	4. b	5. d	6. d	7. d	8. d	9. a	10. a
11. a	12. c	13. d	14. c	15. d	16. c	17. d	18. d	19. b	20. d
21. a	22. d	23. d	24. d	25. a	26. d	27. a	28. d		

Chapter 6
1. d	2. a	3. d	4. c	5. d	6. d	7. d	8. d	9. d	10. d
11. d	12. a	13. a	14. d	15. a	16. d	17. b	18. d	19. b	20. c
21. c	22. a	23. d	24. d	25. b	26. b	27. d	28. a	29. d	30. b
31. b	32. b	33. d	34. a	35. d	36. d	37. a	38. d	39. d	

Chapter 7
1. d	2. d	3. b	4. a	5. c	6. d	7. b	8. c	9. c	10. a
11. d	12. a	13. c	14. c	15. d	16. b	17. a	18. d	19. b	20. d
21. b	22. b	23. b	24. c	25. d	26. a	27. d	28. d	29. c	30. c
31. d	32. a	33. d	34. d	35. a	36. c	37. a	38. c	39. c	40. d
41. c	42. c	43. d	44. b	45. b	46. a	47. a	48. c	49. b	

Chapter 8

1. a	2. d	3. d	4. a	5. d	6. d	7. c	8. c	9. d	10. d
11. d	12. d	13. d	14. a	15. d	16. d	17. d	18. b	19. c	20. b
21. b	22. b	23. d	24. d	25. a	26. d	27. b	28. a	29. d	30. d
31. d	32. d	33. d	34. d	35. d	36. d	37. d	38. d	39. d	40. d
41. c	42. d	43. b	44. d	45. d	46. a	47. b	48. d	49. c	50. d
51. c	52. c	53. c	54. d	55. d	56. d	57. d	58. d	59. d	60. d

Chapter 9

1. c	2. d	3. d	4. a	5. d	6. d	7. d	8. b	9. d	10. d
11. d	12. a	13. d	14. d	15. d	16. c	17. d	18. d	19. d	20. d
21. c	22. d	23. d							

www.ingramcontent.com/pod-product-compliance
Lightning Source LLC
Chambersburg PA
CBHW082044230426
43670CB00016B/2776